HOME PLANNERS COMPLETE BOOK OF
LANDSCAPE PLANS

HOME PLANNERS COMPLETE BOOK OF
LANDSCAPE PLANS

Published by Home Planners, LLC
Wholly owned by Hanley-Wood, LLC

President, Jayne Fenton
Chief Financial Officer, Joe Carroll
Vice President, Publishing, Jennifer Pearce
Vice President, Retail Sales, Chuck Tripp
Vice President, General Manager, Marc Wheeler
Executive Editor, Linda Bellamy
National Sales Manager, Book Division, Julie Marshall
Managing Editor, Jason D. Vaughan
Special Projects Editor, Kristin Schneidler
Associate Editors, Nate Ewell, Kathryn R. Sears
Lead Plans Associate, Morenci C. Clark
Plans Associates, Jill M. Hall, Elizabeth Landry, Nick Nieskes
Proofreaders/Copywriters, Douglas Jenness, Sarah Lyons
Technical Specialist, Jay C. Walsh
Lead Data Coordinator, Fran Altemose
Data Coordinators, Misty Boler, Melissa Siewert
Production Director, Sara Lisa
Production Manager, Brenda McClary

Big Designs, Inc.
President, Creative Director, Anthony D'Elia
Vice President, Business Manager, Megan D'Elia
Vice President, Design Director, Chris Bonavita
Editorial Director, John Roach
Assistant Editor, Tricia Starkey
Director of Design and Production, Stephen Reinfurt
Group Art Director, Kevin Limongelli
Photo Editor, Christine DiVuolo
Art Director, Jessica Hagenbuch
Graphic Designer, Mary Ellen Mulshine
Graphic Designer, Lindsey O'Neill-Myers
Assistant Photo Editor, Mark Storch
Project Director, David Barbella
Assistant Production Manager, Rich Fuentes

Portions of this book were adapted from previous titles: *The Backyard Landscaper, Beds & Borders, Easy-Care Landscape Plans,* and *The Home Landscaper* by Susan A. Roth & Company.

Susan A. Roth & Company
3 Lamont Lane
Stony Brook, New York 11790
Publisher, Susan A. Roth

Landscape Designs by: Ireland-Gannon Associates, Inc.
Rt. 25A, Northern Blvd.
East Norwich, New York 11732

Landscape Renderings by Ray Skibinski
Landscape Plot Plans by Damon Scott and Michael Iragorri
Do-it-Yourself Plans in Chapter 1 by Gordon Morrison

Home Planners Corporate Headquarters
3275 W. Ina Road, Suite 220
Tucson, Arizona 85741

Distribution Center
29333 Lorie Lane
Wixom, Michigan 48393

© 2003

10 9 8 7 6 5 4 3 2 1

Printed in the United States of America

Library of Congress Control Number: 2003113852

ISBN softcover: 1-931131-21-X

102

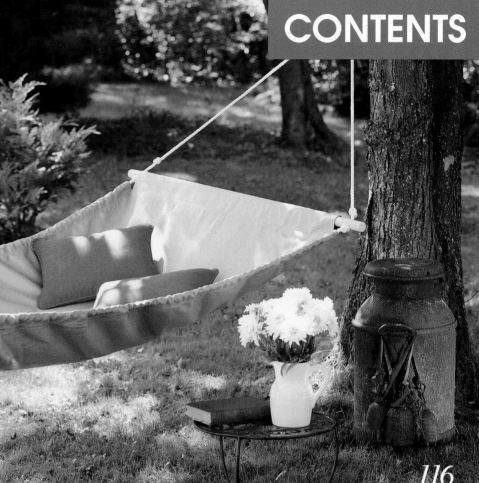

116

32

130

CONTENTS

HOME PLANNERS COMPLETE BOOK OF

LANDSCAPE PLANS

CHAPTER 1

Get Professional Results in Your Yard

Bright colors. Enchanting aromas. And the promise of peace and tranquility.

You'll find all those things and more in *Home Planners Complete Book of Landscape Plans*. Complete blueprints are available, including detailed maps and regionalized plant lists, for each of the plans featured in Chapters 2 through 10. Turn to page 153 for blueprint ordering information.

The designs in this book are conveniently organized with chapters focusing on specific types of landscapes, like flower gardens (Chapter 3) or shade gardens (Chapter 6). Specific features are also highlighted, like water features (Chapter 7) or children's play areas (Chapter 10).

In addition to the plans, you'll find tips and advice throughout the book to help you make your yard everything you hoped it could be. In the next eight pages you'll find invaluable maintenance techniques, plus four small-scale designs you can use in your yard today!

By using one of the plans in this book—whether you install it yourself or hire a contractor—you can be assured that you are getting a top-quality design created by award-winning horticulturists and landscape designers. Landscaping is an investment in the enjoyment and value of your home—this book will help you make the most of that investment.

RIGHT: Tulips are an elegant option for a spring-blooming flower. Here tall lily-flowered tulips create see-through color beside a patio.

ABOVE RIGHT: Double daffodils offer an unusual change from the traditional early spring bloomers. ABOVE: Lamb's Ears provide a silver carpet beneath Dutch hyacinths.

nance, and there are several key steps you can take to ensure the health and beauty of your new landscape:

- Watering
- Preventing Weeds
- Mulching
- Managing Pests and Diseases
- Caring for Plants, Trees, and Shrubs

WATERING

Few climates can provide the consistent moisture on a weekly basis that most gardens require. Most plants can go for a few days without water, but many begin to go dormant, lose roots, and even die if drought lasts for a few weeks or more. Gardeners must step in and irrigate landscape plants when necessary.

It's better to water infrequently but deeply—say, one good soaking a week—than to apply small amounts of water every few days. Apply enough water to penetrate the soil about 18 inches. Wetting only the soil surface weakens plants by encouraging shallow, drought-vulnerable roots to form.

You can reduce the number of waterings by working organic matter, such as compost or leaf mold, into the soil to improve its moisture retention. Adding organic matter is especially beneficial in the case of sandy soils, which have a low organic content and do not retain water well.

To determine if a plant needs water, the time-tested method is to stick your

MAINTENANCE TIPS AND TECHNIQUES

It doesn't take a green thumb—or extensive work—to create a gorgeous garden. Creating natural beauty begins with the design, and the plans in this book are the first step in that direction. But every garden requires basic mainte-

CURB APPEAL

This colorful planting around a mailbox would brighten any front yard. You'll find more elaborate plans with Curb Appeal in Chapter 2, beginning on page 14.

Plant List
1. *Veronica prostrata* (Veronica)
2. *Veronica spicata* (Spike speedwell)
3. *Coreopsis verticillata* (Threadleaf coreopsis)
4. *Stachys byzantina* (Lamb's ears)
5. *Salvia officinalis* (Sage)
6. *Echinacea purpurea* (Purple coneflower)
7. *Perovskia atriplicifolia* (Azure sage)

finger within the plant's root zone. In the case of most annuals and shallow-rooted perennials, it's probably time to water if the soil feels dry an inch below the surface. This method works, but if your garden is large, you may want to use a stick instead of your finger.

Here's another trick for telling at a glance if your garden needs watering: within each group of plants, include one or more "indicator" plants, such as phlox, that you know wilt quickly when the soil dries out. As you make the rounds in your garden, pay special attention to the indicator plants and give them—and the plants growing nearby—a drink as soon as they start to droop.

PREVENTING WEEDS

Bare soil is at the mercy of drying sunlight and erosion caused by wind and rain, so nature protects the soil by covering it with plants. Unwanted plants, or weeds, will pop up in any garden site that you leave bare.

Fight weeds effectively—before they appear—by:

■ Covering garden soil with weed-smothering mulch.

■ Planting a dense group of low-growing groundcovers beneath trees and shrubs, and even under perennials and bulbs.

■ Laying down plastic sheeting, landscape fabric, or several sheets of newspaper beneath a gravel or mulch path.

If a few weeds poke up through the mulch or groundcover, they will be easy to hand-pull when the soil is moist from rain or watering. If stubborn perennial weeds keep coming back from underground runners, try pouring boiling water on their roots.

Weeds can be killed with the systemic herbicide glyphosate, which is sold under various trade names. This herbicide remains in the plant's tissues and does not move through the soil. It also breaks down quickly, so it is relatively safe to use.

When using any herbicide, follow the label directions carefully. Use only on wind-free days, and take care not to splash it on desirable plants, because most herbicides kill plants indiscriminately.

MULCHING

Mulching is probably the easiest of all garden chores, and possibly the best thing you can do for your garden. Mulch is a layer of organic or inorganic material placed on the soil beneath plants. Mulch smothers weeds, thus reducing the need for weeding, and it helps keep the soil moist, which saves on watering.

A 2- to 4-inch layer of loose material insulates the soil, protecting surface roots from heat during the summer and from frost damage and heaving during the winter. Mulch also protects plants from diseases by keeping soil-bourne pathogens from splashing onto leaves.

Organic mulches, such as compost, wood chips, shredded leaves, and aged manure, slowly release valuable nutrients into the soil, reducing the need for fertilizing. Compost also adds beneficial,

TOP: Crocus can provide a mix of color early in the spring, adding interest to your yard just as the weather warms up. ABOVE: This orange meadowbright coneflower features a rich color and will grow between 15 and 24 inches high in full sun.

Landscape fabrics are not meant to be used alone, but can be placed under loose mulches for added weed suppression. Use landscape fabric under trees and shrubs only where you intend the covering to be permanent. If you try to remove fabric under trees or shrubs you may damage surface roots—they sometimes weave themselves into the fabric.

MANAGING PESTS AND DISEASES

Selecting disease- and insect-resistant plants—such as the ones showcased in this book—and keeping them healthy can help you avoid trouble with pests and diseases. Healthy plants are less likely to suffer these problems, since pests and diseases naturally seek out weaker victims. By simply providing plants with the type of soil, drainage, nutrients, and moisture they require, you'll help strengthen them so they can survive an occasional attack.

Many of the routine maintenance techniques described in this chapter—like watering deeply and mulching—help make plants strong enough to resist pest and disease attacks. A few other simple steps can help you avoid a problem down the road.

First, wash plants off regularly with a vigorous spray of water from the hose, making sure to hit both upper and lower sides of leaves. This actually knocks off tiny insects and disease spores. Spray plants in the morning so that they have time to dry by sundown; many diseases thrive on foliage that stays wet overnight, when the air is cool.

It's also helpful to keep your garden clean by removing dead leaves and other plant debris. This not only keeps the garden tidy, but also eliminates a favorite breeding ground for all sorts of pests and diseases—and gives you the makings for great compost.

Even well-maintained gardens with healthy plants have occasional problems. If a few leaves are spotted with fuzzy, white, or sooty, black fungal spots, simply pick and destroy them to keep the

disease-fighting organisms to the soil.

When using fresh organic mulches, add nitrogen-rich fertilizers to the area to replenish the nutrients these mulches use as they decompose. Because organic mulches break down, you'll need to refresh the mulch every year or so. Add a layer of new mulch in the spring or early summer to maintain a depth between 2 and 4 inches.

Inorganic mulches include synthetic landscape fabrics, crushed rock, or gravel. These mulches suppress weeds, but offer little insulation and no nutrients for plant roots—they can also cook some plants. Crushed rock and gravel look best when used to cover paths or large, unplanted areas, or placed around plants in rock gardens and arid landscapes.

problem from spreading. Pick off large leaf-chewing pests with gloved hands and drop them into a jar of soapy water.

If the damage threatens your plants' health, identify the culprits and take appropriate action. Check with your local garden center for remedies to specific problems, or snip off an affected leaf and take it to your local cooperative extension agent to identify the critters and get treatment options.

CARING FOR PLANTS, TREES, & SHRUBS

Once you've installed your landscape, take care of its plants. Generally, you'll need to pay a bit more attention to herbaceous plants than woody plants, since the former require deadheading and fertilizing. You'll also want to prune woody plants to keep them looking their best for years to come. Some general plant care guidelines follow; for care of specific plants, consult your local nursery.

Once established, trees and shrubs require minimal attention to thrive. Generally, all you'll need to do is prune them from time to time to maintain their shape and health. Trees and shrubs usually don't require nutrients beyond what the soil supplies, but any organic mulch or fertilizer you add to your garden will help.

Winter is the best time to prune most trees and shrubs. In the late winter, your landscape may look like it's still asleep, but it's on the verge of bursting into buds, flowers, and leaves. It's much easier to prune deciduous trees before this new growth begins, since you can see where you're cutting more clearly.

You can prune summer-flowering shrubs and trees in late winter or early spring without sacrificing flowers, because the flower buds form during the present growing season. Wait to prune spring bloomers, such as forsythias, quinces, and lilacs, until after they bloom so you won't lose the flowers, which develop from over-wintering buds. Don't wait too long,

though; if you prune in the late summer or fall, you may cut off next year's flower buds.

PERENNIAL CARE

When caring for perennials, you will need to fertilize, divide, deadhead, and possibly stake or support them—each at different times during their life span.

Fertilizers have varying proportions of the three major elements that plants need for healthy growth: nitrogen, phosphorus, and potassium (abbreviated as N-P-K). The proportion of N-P-K is noted on the label as a series of numbers, such as 5-10-5, which is a good formula for perennials.

Apply a balanced slow-release fertilizer in late spring by scattering the pellets on the surface of the soil and scratching

it in lightly. Rain and irrigation water will slowly leach nutrients from the pellets into the soil. Your perennials won't need more fertilizer until they bloom later in the summer, and this one application will be enough for foliage plants.

Weak-stemmed plants—or those in windy sites—may need to be staked as the season progresses to support their growth. Anticipate the problem in the spring and stick stakes or metal grids into the soil where floppy perennials, such as peonies, are emerging. If you install the support early in the growing season, the plant's leaves will grow up and around to camouflage the support.

Another easy way to provide support is to plant vines or floppy plants, like clematis

ISLAND GARDEN

The larger Calamagrostis acutiflora (reed grass) anchors this island planting, but it's the colorful flowers that really bring it alive. Add it to your yard or turn to Chapter 3, beginning on page 32, for more elaborate flower garden plans.

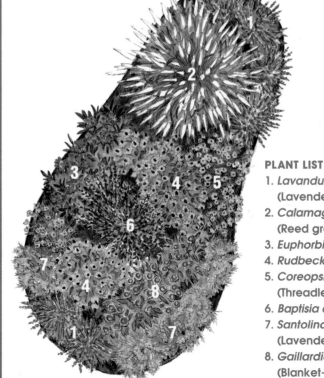

PLANT LIST
1. *Lavandula angustifolia* (Lavender)
2. *Calamagrostis acutiflora* (Reed grass)
3. *Euphorbia graffithii* (Spurge)
4. *Rudbeckia hirta* (Coneflower)
5. *Coreopsis verticillata* (Threadleaf coreopsis)
6. *Baptisia australis* (Wild indigo)
7. *Santolina chamaecyparissus* (Lavender cotton)
8. *Gaillardia x grandiflora* (Blanket-flower)

ABOVE: Keeping your tools clean and well organized saves effort in the long run, and can extend the lifespan of your garden tools.

or balloon flowers, with stiff plants, like shrub roses. By allowing the vines or floppy plants to wind through or lean on the stronger plants, you can save yourself the work of staking and enjoy handsome combinations of flower colors at the same time.

When flowers begin to fade, keep the plants looking tidy and encourage more flowers by deadheading, or removing old blossoms. Use pruning shears or scissors to remove individual faded flowers near the main stem. You can remove tall, leafless flower stems, such as those of iris, at the base.

While you wait for most of your plants to awaken in early spring, spring-flowering bulbs are in their glory. Apply nitrogen-rich fertilizer just as the new foliage pokes though the ground, and you will fuel their growth, and help bulbs store food for strong blooming performance next spring. In the fall, apply bulb booster fertilizer, a balanced slow-release plant food, to help the bulbs grow a good root system.

If you've done all you can to keep your bulbs and perennials healthy, they will thrive. New plants will form around the original clumps. Typically, after three to five years, the clumps become crowded, the centers begin to die out, and flower production decreases. When this happens, you'll need to dig the clumps up in spring or fall and divide them into individual plants. Discard the spent, old plants at the center and replant the new ones.

PUTTING GARDENS TO BED

Fall, like spring, is a busy time in the garden. Dusting the soil above spring-flowering bulbs with fertilizer again in autumn will give them an energy boost when they revive in the spring. And, of course, you'll want to plant new bulbs in the fall as well.

If you have precious tender plants that you'd like to save for next summer, now's the time to dig them up and put them in pots to bring indoors. Find a bright, sunny windowsill for the winter and they'll be ready to go back outside in the spring.

Autumn is the time to protect plants from frost damage. Applying a 4-inch-thick layer of fresh mulch after the ground freezes will keep plants from being heaved from the soil. If you have shrubs that are exposed to drying winds, you can protect them by wrapping them in burlap or spraying the leaves or needles with an antidessicant, available at garden centers. Wait to apply this product until temperatures fall below freezing so that you're sure that plants are dormant before you treat them.

If you are growing herbs, vegetables, or late-flowering annuals and want to keep them going as long as possible, cover them with old bedsheets or synthetic floating row covers in the evening when frost threatens. Pull the coverings off in the morning.

Late winter is the time to cut back ornamental grasses and any perennials that you left in the garden for winter interest. Using a pair of hand shears, cut back grasses and perennials to an inch or two above the base of each plant. If the dried foliage you've removed is free of insects and disease, you can compost the clippings.

THE RIGHT TOOLS

No matter what time of year you're doing landscape chores, you'll save time and effort if you are equipped with quality tools. Whenever possible, shop for hand tools in a store, rather than by mail. That way, you can try them on, much as you would try on a pair of shoes. If you're buying a shovel, for example, take one off the rack and see how it fits. If it's too heavy or too tall, chances are you'll never use it.

For smaller adults, look for lightweight tools designed for women—often they

BUTTERFLY GARDEN

This beautiful planting will provide endless enjoyment not only for you and your guests, but also for butterflies. They'll love the flowers chosen in this design. Find complete landscapes designed with nature in mind in Chapter 4, beginning on page 46.

PLANT LIST

1. *Buddleia davidii* (Butterfly bush)
2. *Abelia x grandiflora* (Abelia)
3. *Echinacea purpurea* (Purple coneflower)
4. *Asclepias tuberosa* (Milkweed)
5. *Eupatorium maculatum* (Joe-Pye Weed)
6. *Aster x frikartii* (Aster)
7. *Sedum spectabile* (Stonecrop)
8. *Monarda didyma* (Wild bergamot)
9. *Petunia x hybrida* (Petunia)
10. *Scabiosa caucasica* (Pincushion flower)
11. *Aster x nova-angliae* (Aster)

can be a better choice. Good tools last a lifetime or two, and you can often find high-quality, hand-forged garden tools at bargain prices. Keep an eye out at thrift shops and yard sales for the best deals.

SELECTING YOUR HARDSCAPE

The paving, fences, walls, and any garden ornaments used in a landscape design are often called the hardscape, while the plant materials are called the softscape. The hardscape plays an important role in any design, contributing line, pattern, form, color, and texture.

Well-designed landscapes use paving materials for driveways and walkways that have colors, textures, and patterns that complement the construction material of the house. Some materials, like concrete, brick, or stone, can be used in both driveways and walkways, but this is not always possible since the driveway needs to support more weight than a walkway. Wood, for example, is rarely used on a driveway,

but works well on paths if the house is by the coast or has a naturalistic, weather-beaten look. In that type of situation, you could edge the driveway in the same wood as the path to unify the two.

Bricks are available in different textures and colors and can be used on driveways, walkways, patios, and steps. Used bricks are rougher in texture and therefore more suitable for walkways. You don't need to embed bricks in mortar or concrete unless cars will be driving on them, although mortar or concrete gives them more permanence and keeps out weeds. Alternatively, lay bricks in a 2-inch base of sand, then brush more sand on top until the cracks between the bricks are filled.

ABOVE: Proper care will help your tulips grow tall, strong, and bright. Applying bulb booster fertilizer in the fall will help them establish a good root base.

Plant and fertilize bulbs such as daffodils in the early fall.

GARDEN TASK PLANNER

EARLY SPRING
■ **Fertilize bulbs with N-P-K**
Early application of commercial or organic fertilizer fuels fast growth and feeds bulbs for next year's flowers

LATE SPRING
■ **Prune, deadhead**
Use hand shears, loppers, or a pruning saw; thin spring-flowering shrubs after flowers fade; deadhead most bulbs, allowing only species bulbs to set seed
■ **Divide perennials**
Use a spade or garden fork; multiply plants without buying new ones by dividing overgrown clumps; this will increase flowering and maintain health
■ **Prepare new beds**
Use a garden fork, shovel, garden rake, and compost; apply amendments with a shovel, turn soil with a fork, and break up clods and level soil with a garden rake
■ **Fertilize perennials, annuals**
Spread balanced, slow-release fertilizer granules or time-release pellets to ensure healthy plants with plentiful flowers

EARLY SUMMER
■ **Bring plants back outside**
Wait until the soil warms after the last frost and plant nursery plants or annuals started indoors from seed
■ **Apply mulch**
Use compost, leaf mold, gravel, bark chips, pine needles, or grass clippings to suppress weeds and keep soil moist and cool

SUMMER
■ **Support plants**
Use stakes or combine plants for support; plant floppy plants and vines next to sturdy plants to save work later
■ **Control weeds**
Use a hoe or hand cultivator, hand-pull, or smother with a barrier
■ **Deadhead**
Use lightweight pruning shears to remove spent flowers and encourage rebloom
■ **Irrigate during dry periods**
Use watering devices attached to timers to save effort and irrigate more effectively
■ **Battle bugs and diseases**
Identify problems early; good garden hygiene and a watchful eye save money and plant health
■ **Edge beds and borders**
Use an edging tool or sharp spade to slice through sod and remove grass roots from bed edges

EARLY AUTUMN
■ **Plant bulbs**
Use a spade or narrow-bladed trowel to dig holes and place several bulbs side-by-side for natural looking drifts
■ **Fertilize bulbs**
Use bulb-booster fertilizer to encourage healthy root formation

LATE AUTUMN
■ **Overwinter tender plants**
Use hand shears, pots, potting soil, and a trowel to take cuttings or dig up treasured plants and bring them indoors for the winter
■ **Clean up garden**
Use hand pruners and a leaf rake to remove and compost plant debris, which protects plants by removing overwintering sites for pests and diseases

EARLY WINTER
■ **Mulch**
Apply fresh mulch once the soil is frozen to prevent heaving

LATE WINTER
■ **Prune shrubs**
Use hand shears, loppers, or a pruning saw; remove dead and damaged branches, and prune woody plants that bloom in summer
■ **Cut back grasses, perennials**
Use hedge shears or a string trimmer; cut dead plants back to a couple of inches above ground before they send up new growth
■ **Order seeds and plants**
Explore mail-order garden catalogs; you'll get more plants and more interesting cultivars than simply visiting your local nursery.

Concrete is one of the most inexpensive paving materials, although not always the most attractive. It can be laid in any shape, and may be the easiest way to deal with a circular design. Be aware that smooth concrete is slippery when wet; a textured finish is safer and can be made more attractive with a sweeping circular design. Adding heavy aggregate to concrete strengthens it and makes it more attractive, as does dividing it into sections broken up with pieces of treated wood. Concrete can also be beautified by coloring it, stamping it, or topping it with colored stones.

Pre-cast interlocking concrete pavers are strong and easy to install. They come in a variety of shapes, textures, and colors, and while more expensive than concrete, they are more economical than brick, flagstone, slate, or other stones.

Quarried stones such as granite, marble, bluestone, and slate are often used as paving materials. Dimensioned stone, since it is cut, is easy to work with because it is usually flat. You can also use fieldstone, but you'll need to take care when laying the stone to ensure that the surface is flat and easy to walk on.

Pressure-treated lumber has preservative forced deep into the wood and lasts longer than wood that has simply been dipped or painted with preservative. Pressure-treated wood is not toxic to plants and the preservatives will not leach into the soil; however, use extreme caution when sawing the wood to prevent inhaling or ingesting the dust particles. ■

BELOW: A fence and tall grasses can add depth, height, and focal points to a landscape.

LATE SUMMER GARDEN

Tucked amid bright blues and violets, with a stunning backdrop of roses, this is the perfect place to enjoy a cool glass of lemonade. Find landscapes for your entire backyard that feature similar quiet retreats in Chapter 9, beginning on page 116.

PLANT LIST
1. *Buddleia davidii* (Butterfly bush)
2. *Artemisia absinthium* (Wormwood)
3. *Thymus praecox* (Thyme)
4. *Nepeta x faassenii* (Catmint)
5. *Campanula carpatica* (Bellflower)
6. *Rose "Constance spry"* (Climbing rose)
7. *Lavandula angustifolia* (Lavender)
8. *Calamintha nepeta* (Calamint)

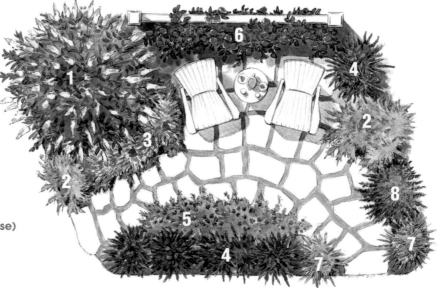

CHAPTER 2

Curb Appeal

Landscapes for Front Yards

Create a well-designed front yard and you'll have the perfect place to come home to every day—as well as an inviting welcome to visiting friends and family. An attractive transition from curb to front door will enhance both the beauty and the value of your home.

Front yard designs can serve a number of purposes—from welcoming guests and neighbors to your home to providing privacy from the street. Whatever your goals, the designs in this book can help you achieve them, since they are created by landscape architects using time-tested design principles.

A landscape professional would ask you some important questions before beginning any type of design, but you can go through the process yourself as you flip through this book. Ask yourself these questions, writing down your answers and making lists if you wish:

■ How much time do you have to tend to a garden?

■ What are the growing conditions where

you want to install your new plan?

■ What is your personal style and the style of your house: casual or formal? Bold or subdued?

Those answers will help you create the perfect design for your landscape—not just in the front yard, which is the focus of this chapter, but in the back as well.

YOUR SITE

As you look at your yard, determine the location and the amount of space you plan to allocate for your design. Carry a tape

RIGHT: A spiked plant can provide height in a design, as well as a focal point that will direct visitors towards the home's entrance.

Comprehensive blueprint packages are available for each of the designs in this chapter. Professionally designed and prepared with attention to detail, these easy-to-follow plans include:

■ a precise plot plan

■ regionalized plant and materials lists

■ a plant size and description guide

■ installation and maintenance information

These plans will help you or your contractor achieve professional results, adding beauty and value to your property for years. Turn to page 153 for ordering information.

measure and notepad to jot down measurements and take notes. Take photos from the vantage points from which you will actually view the new garden: from the patio, from the front walkway, from the kitchen window, etc. A photograph can show you things you might not have noticed on a walking tour of the property.

Once you get the photos developed, spread them out and take a critical look. Does one corner of the yard look bare? Does another area need to have a tree or two removed? You can even draw right on the photos with a grease pencil to experiment with any landscape changes that you're considering.

Next assess the amount of sunlight and quality of the soil in the chosen site. If you're removing an existing garden to make way for the new design, note the types of plants that thrived in the area, as well as ones that seemed to struggle.

Observe the path of the sun over the course of the day as it relates to your garden site. Look for shade cast by existing trees, your house, or nearby structures, including fences. You may find that the area gets full sun in the morning, but the neighbor's fence casts a shadow the rest of the day. Remember, also, that the angle of the sun is different in the summer than in winter.

DESIGN PRINCIPLES

A sense of visual rhythm in a landscape invites your eye to move along the expanse of the garden in a leisurely manner, while at the same time encouraging you to view the entire design as a whole. Landscape designers establish a sense of visual rhythm by alternating strong design elements with more delicate ones, and by repeating colors and drifts—or groups—of plants.

For example, you can plant several drifts of tall pink tulips and sweet woodruff at roughly equal distances from each other along the length and width of a property border. This kind of repetition of color and texture provides a visually pleasing sense of organization. To create effective drifts, group odd numbers of at least three plants together. Smaller perennials and bulbs look better in drifts of five or nine—using generous amounts of plants in each drift helps avoid a polka-dot effect across your yard.

Landscape designers create balanced plans by siting elements according to their color, texture, and size, as well as their visual mass or weight. Creating a formal, symmetrical design is one way to achieve balance, or you can develop an informal—but still balanced—plan. For example, a long, curving border may have a small gazebo at one end, balanced on the other end by an ornamental tree or group of shrubs with the same visual mass.

ADD A FOCAL POINT

Nothing in a landscape catches the eye and imagination as much as a partly obscured garden bench or gazebo peeking out from behind a curtain of flowering vines. Even completely visible garden furnishings—such as benches, stone walls, birdbaths, garden statues, arbors, trellises, and fountains—tend to draw attention to them-

LEFT: The repetition of various groups of flowering plants establishes a sense of visual rhythm within this yard.

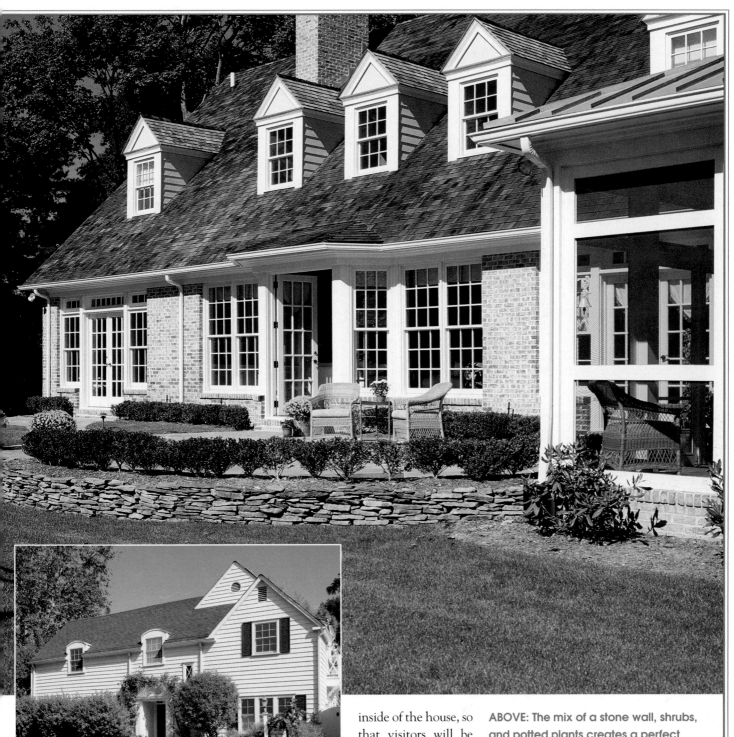

ABOVE: The mix of a stone wall, shrubs, and potted plants creates a perfect welcome. LEFT: Stretching above the front door, plant life plays an integral role in your first impression of this house.

inside of the house, so that visitors will be drawn to the surrounding garden. The same garden furnishings you use to create focal points also function as permanent structural elements, especially during the colder months when perennials are out of bloom and deciduous trees are leafless.

Larger plants, such as flowering trees and shrubs, tall perennials, and ornamental grasses, also make effective focal points. Place a single specimen plant in a mixed bed

selves. People perceive these focal points as destinations and instinctively want to take a closer look. The stone path leading to the backyard in our Classic Colonial design (page 24) is a perfect example.

For maximum impact, site benches, arbors, and other furnishings where they can be seen from a distance, or from the

or border where it can act as a exclamation mark to the design or to visually anchor the garden. Focal points, whether they are softscape or hardscape elements, are most intriguing when they are placed either centrally in a design or noticeably off center. Objects or plants that are only slightly off center tend to look unbalanced. ■

CLASSIC LANDSCAPE

plan # HPT94001

SHOWN IN SPRING
DESIGN BY JEFFERY DIEFENBACH

SEE PAGE 153 TO ORDER OUR COMPREHENSIVE BLUEPRINT PACKAGE, INCLUDING A REGIONALIZED PLANT AND MATERIALS LIST AND OTHER INVALUABLE INFORMATION TO HELP YOU CREATE THIS LANDSCAPE.

This easy-care landscape contains graceful shade trees, compact shrubs, and an assortment of colorful perennials and bulbs. Weed-free flagstones and cobblestones complement the home's wood siding.

Plan View

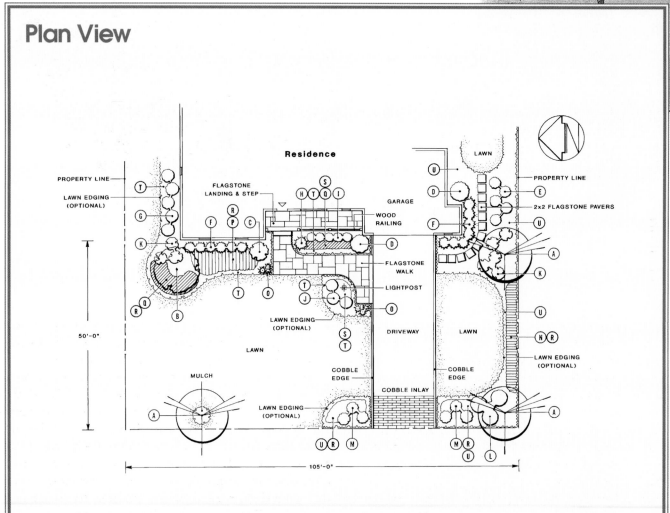

This classic house style, with its steep roofline and tidy clapboards, demands a traditional, shade-tree-filled landscape. Fulfilling that function is a trio of elegantly branching deciduous trees. A specimen tree in the foundation planting on the left of the house provides dramatic spring blossoms and summer shade.

The trees and shrubs in the beds are underplanted with groundcovers, perennials, and bulbs. All the plants in the design are chosen for ease of care and for their attractive foliage, flowers, or fruit. For instance, the clusters of tough bronze-leaved shrubs flanking the foot of the drive provide eye-catching color most of the year and remain low enough so they won't block a driver's view. The foundation plantings contain compact plants that won't block the windows or the decorative wooden porch railing. The planting pocket marking the front walk holds low plants that won't engulf the lamp-post or obscure light from the lamp.

The designer chooses flagstones and cobblestones to complement the home's traditional clapboards. Flagstones in the walk and on the porch landing are mortared for weed-free upkeep, while the pavers leading around the garage are set in groundcover. The cobble inlay visually extends the plantings across the drive, and the edging serves as a mowing strip. The patches of lawn on both sides of the drive are designed for fast mowing. The ring of mulch under the tree protects the trunk and eliminates the need to hand trim. Also shown here is home plan HPB947 by Home Planners. For information about ordering blueprints for this home, call 1-800-521-6797.

COUNTRY-STYLE FARMHOUSE

Set in a friendly and homey landscape brimming with flowers from spring through fall, this farmhouse's country atmosphere is now complete. Masses of perennials and bulbs used throughout the property create a garden setting and provide armloads of flowers that can be cut for indoor bouquets. But the floral beauty doesn't stop there; the designer artfully incorporates unusual specimens of summer- and fall-blooming trees and shrubs into the landscape design to elevate the changing floral scene to eye-level and above.

To match the informal mood of the house, both the front walkway and driveway cut a curved, somewhat meandering path. A parking spur at the end of the driveway provides extra parking space and a place to turn around. Fieldstones, whose rustic character complements the country setting, pave the front walk. The stone piers and picket fence at the entrance to the driveway frame the entry and match the detail and character of the house's stone foundation and porch railing. The stone wall at the side of the property further carries out this theme.

Large specimen trees planted in the lawn set the house back from the road and provide a show of autumn color. Imagine completing the country theme in this tranquil setting by hanging a child's swing from the tree nearest the front porch. Also shown here is home plan HPB774 by Home Planners. For information about ordering blueprints for this home, call 1-800-521-6797.

ORDER BLUEPRINTS 24 HOURS, 7 DAYS A WEEK, AT 1-800-521-6797

Plan View

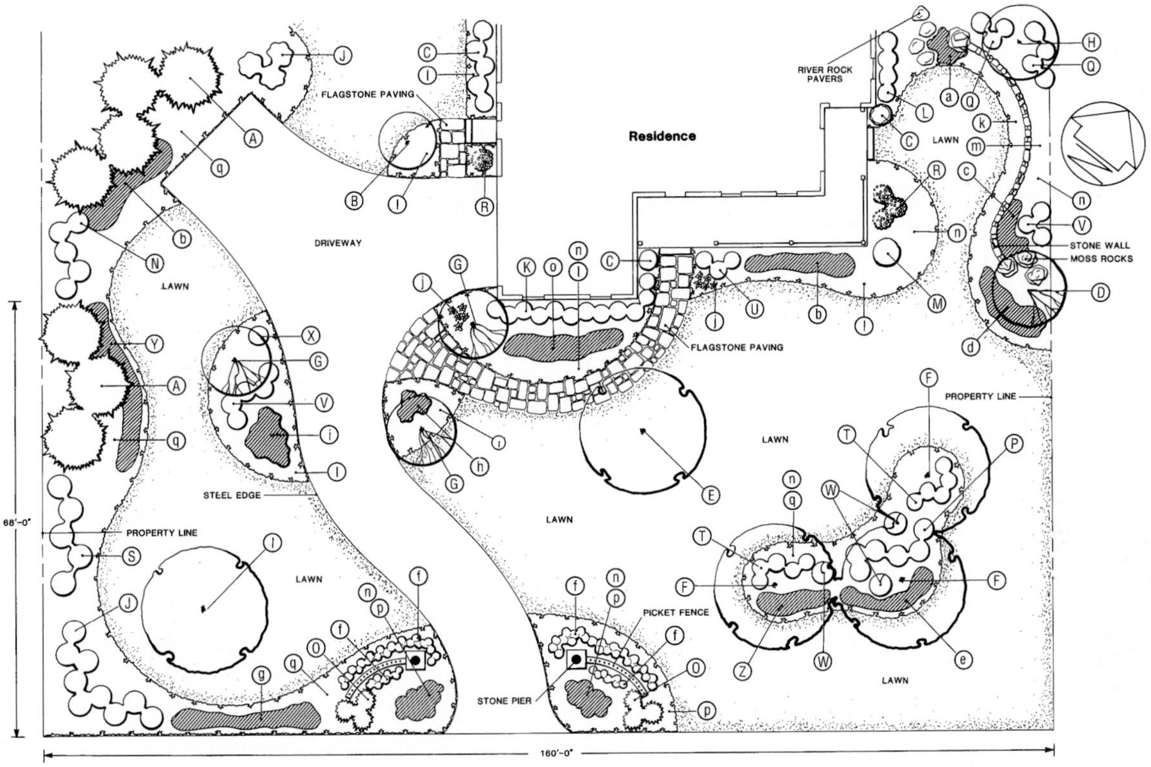

Graceful trees, curving lines and bursts of flowers blooming from spring through fall complement this comfortable country retreat. The friendly landscaping creates the perfect finishing touch that says: here's a place to hang up a hammock and relax.

plan # HPT94002

**SHOWN IN SUMMER
DESIGN BY DAVID POPLAWSKI**

SEE PAGE 153 TO ORDER OUR COMPREHENSIVE BLUEPRINT PACKAGE, INCLUDING A REGIONALIZED PLANT AND MATERIALS LIST AND OTHER INVALUABLE INFORMATION TO HELP YOU CREATE THIS LANDSCAPE.

AMPLIFY A NARROW LOT

plan# HPT94003

**SHOWN IN SUMMER
DESIGN BY DAMON SCOTT**

SEE PAGE 153 TO ORDER OUR COMPREHENSIVE BLUEPRINT PACKAGE, INCLUDING A REGIONALIZED PLANT AND MATERIALS LIST AND OTHER INVALUABLE INFORMATION TO HELP YOU CREATE THIS LANDSCAPE.

The foundation border curving around the house provides the main source of interest in this landscape. However, maintaining it won't tax the easy-care gardener because the plants are compact and disease-resistant.

Plan View

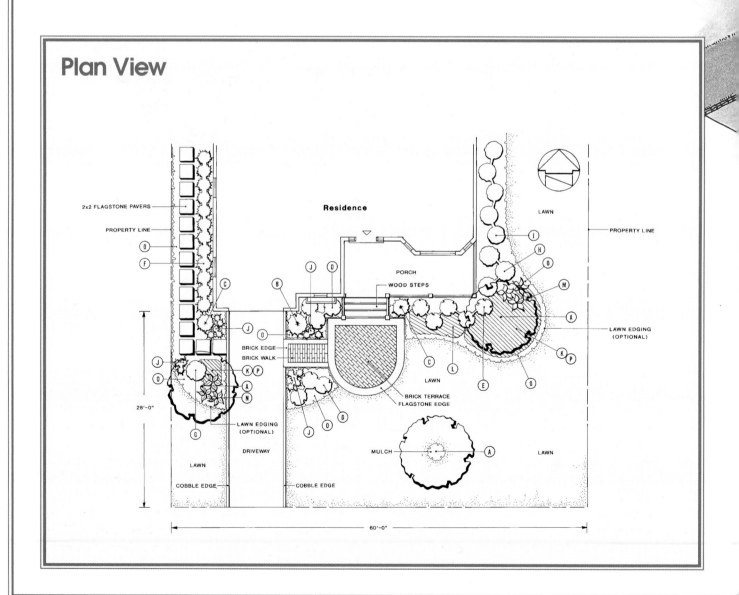

Graceful, curving foundation plantings really make this landscape! Set against a carpet of green grass, the mixed plantings contain shrubs, perennials, bulbs and ground covers chosen for compactness as well as for attractive foliage and flowers. One of a trio of handsome multi-trunked deciduous trees with attractive peeling bark anchors the largest planting. Set near the porch, the tree contributes cool shade during the summer.

The tree to the far left softens the driveway, as do the cobblestones bordering the asphalt. Like the cobbles, the other paving materials—brick and flagstone—are selected for their compatibility with the house style. A brick walk leads to an arching entry landing set at the base of the stairs. The curved landing and planting beds echo the curves in the porch detail and some of the windows. Both the walk and terrace are edged with flagstone, a material repeated in the pavers leading from the opposite side of the driveway to the back of the house.

The third tree in the triangle is planted at the front of the lawn, where its picturesque bark can be admired up close by passersby. At the same time that the tree attracts attention, it also provides some screening and privacy. It is set in a ring of mulch for easy mowing. Also shown here is home plan HPB974 by Home Planners. For information about ordering blueprints for this home, call 1-800-521-6797.

CLASSIC COLONIAL

plan# HPT94004

SHOWN IN SPRING
DESIGN BY MICHAEL J. OPISSO

SEE PAGE 153 TO ORDER OUR COMPREHENSIVE BLUEPRINT PACKAGE, INCLUDING A REGIONALIZED PLANT AND MATERIALS LIST AND OTHER INVALUABLE INFORMATION TO HELP YOU CREATE THIS LANDSCAPE.

The skillful placement of ornamental trees and shrubs in this landscape design frames the walk and front door, leading the eye and visitors past the secondary entrance and directly to the main entrance.

Plan View

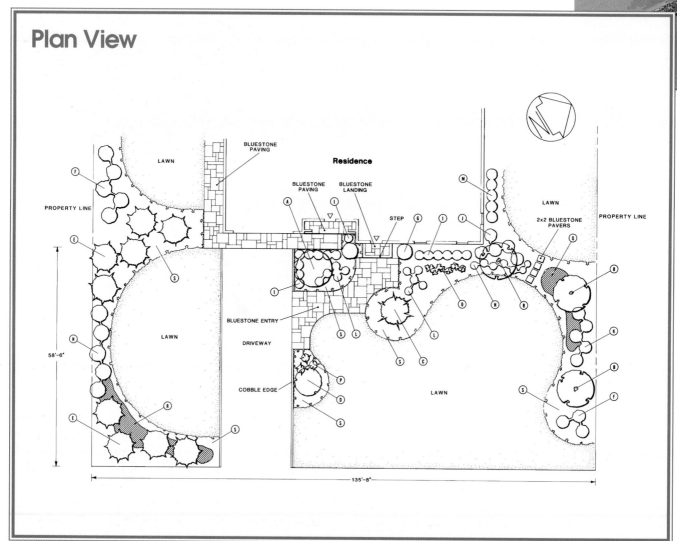

With two entries close to each other at the front of the house, it is imperative that the landscaping for this gambrel-roof Colonial home defines the formal or dominant entry—the one to which a visitor should go. This is accomplished by framing and blocking views.

Notice how small ornamental trees frame the large entry court that leads to the main door. The tree nearest the house blocks the view of the door leading to the family room, and it also frames the walk and adds color and interest to the landscape. A low-growing evergreen hedge behind the tree aids in screening, so the visitor perceives only one walkway and one door. Access to the secondary door from the backyard, garage or driveway is by a walkway at the back of this screen planting.

The weeping evergreen and summer-flowering shrubs bordering the outside of the front walkway direct the view up the walk and to the front door. This bed extends into a curving border of trees, shrubs, perennials and groundcovers, which is echoed on the other side of the property. These border plantings provide privacy from neighbors or a side street and, since one cannot see behind the house, further define the front garden. Also shown here is home plan HPB131 by Home Planners. For information about ordering blueprints for this home, call 1-800-521-6797.

CAPE COD CHARM

Skillful landscaping transforms this ordinary, small Cape Cod house into a cozy, quaint cottage that has instant curb appeal. Relying on an exuberant mix of flowering shrubs and perennials, the design evokes the mood of a friendly country home whose bountiful gardens burst with colorful flowers. Notice how the designer linked the front walk to the driveway with a few pleasing turns and a change of levels rather than dissecting the small property with a front walk leading straight to the street. This layout adds visual interest to the small yard while making it seem broader. The white picket fence adds to the cottage-garden charm while giving the landscape some depth and a feeling of intimacy. Massed together into several large planting beds, graceful trees, flowering shrubs, groundcovers, and perennials border the house and entryway to create an ever-changing informal garden setting. Small boulders add a naturalistic character reminiscent of New England, and also provide a year-round structure to the beds. Planted along the base of the fence, perennials add color during the summer and soften the fence without hiding it. A deciduous shrub with strong spring color highlights the corner of the fenced garden, while evergreen flowering specimens brighten the corners of the house.

Plan View

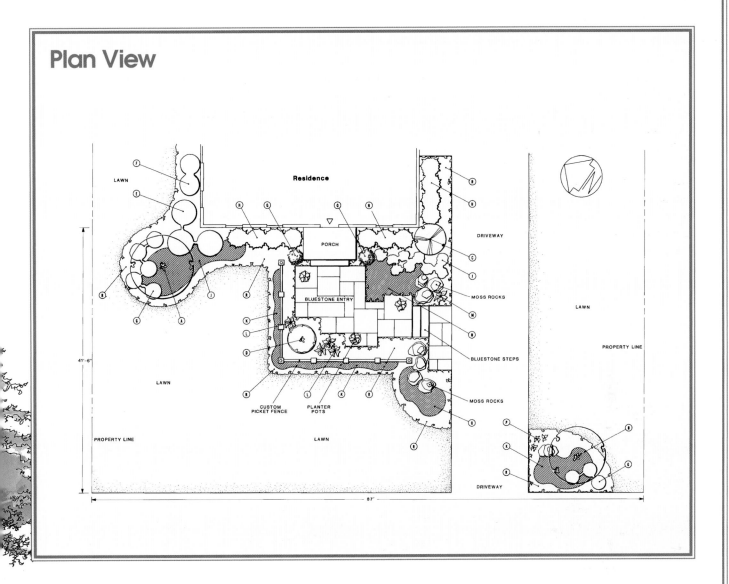

LAWN

Residence

DRIVEWAY

PORCH

BLUESTONE ENTRY

MOSS ROCKS

41'–6"

BLUESTONE STEPS

LAWN

PROPERTY LINE

LAWN

MOSS ROCKS

CUSTOM
PICKET FENCE

PLANTER
POTS

PROPERTY LINE

LAWN

DRIVEWAY

87'

plan ⊕ HPT94005

SHOWN IN SPRING
DESIGN BY SUSAN A. ROTH

SEE PAGE 153 TO ORDER OUR
COMPREHENSIVE BLUEPRINT
PACKAGE, INCLUDING A REGIONAL-
IZED PLANT AND MATERIALS LIST AND
OTHER INVALUABLE INFORMATION TO
HELP YOU CREATE THIS LANDSCAPE.

To balance the weight of the entry bed and paving, the designer placed a small tree and planting bed at the front corner of the driveway. These plants provide a colorful greeting as guests and family members approach the house.

EUROPEAN FLAIR

The designer uses graceful curving borders to bring this landscape to life. An appealing mix of shrubs grown for their ornamental foliage, flowers, and fruit rises from an underplanting of weed-smothering groundcovers and long-blooming perennials. The shrubs' compact growth habits keep the windows clear and save on pruning chores. A small tree, selected for its handsome branching pattern and long season of colorful foliage, partially screens the entry from public view and creates a dramatic focal point. The curves in the borders are repeated in the cobble-edged planting peninsulas, which visually break up the large expanse of asphalt in the drive. Five deciduous shade trees planted along the drive spruce up this utilitarian area while giving needed height to the landscape. The trees are chosen for their airy canopies of delicate leaves, which create a softening screen without excessive shade or fall cleanup. A flagstone walk, set in concrete and mortared for weed-free maintenance, zigzags from the drive to the front porch. For a greater feeling of privacy, the designer ends the walk short of the street so that it is accessible only from the drive.

Plan View

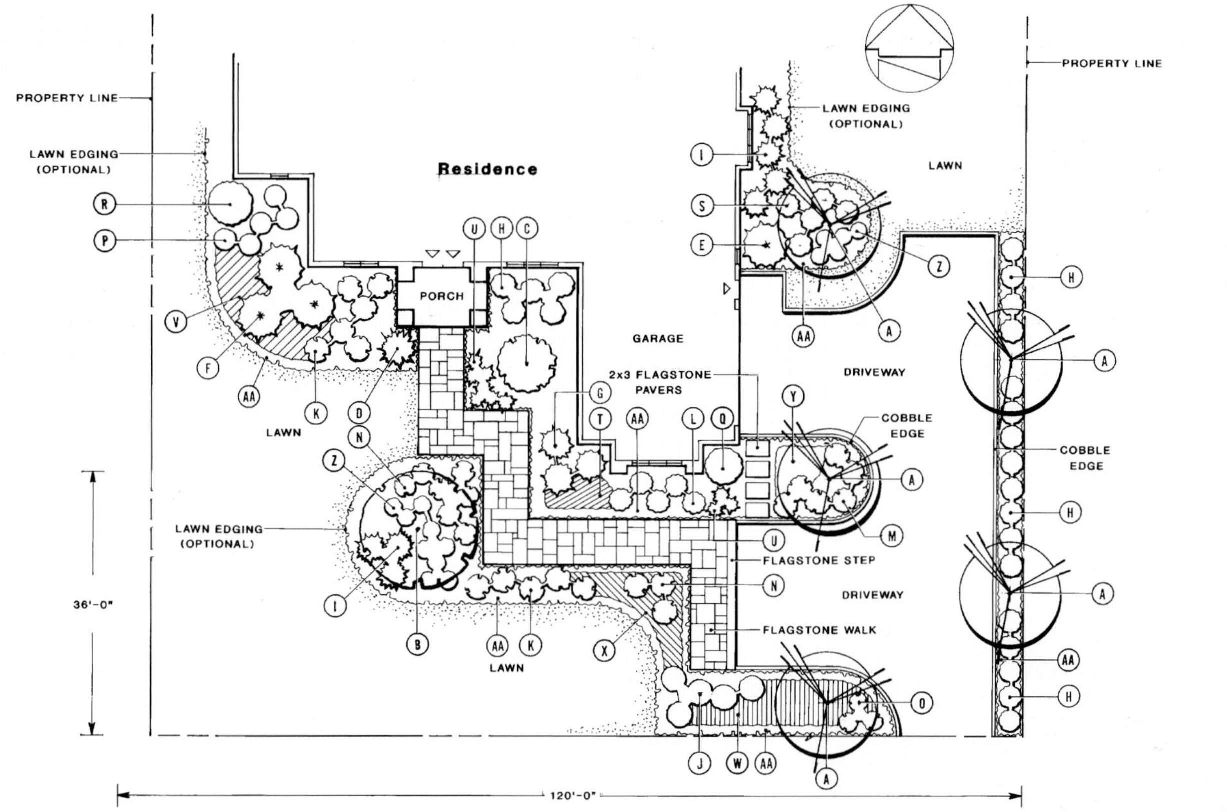

Plan View diagram — Landscape plan showing Residence, Porch, Garage, Driveway, Lawn areas. Labels include:

- PROPERTY LINE
- LAWN EDGING (OPTIONAL)
- Residence
- PORCH
- LAWN
- 2x3 FLAGSTONE PAVERS
- GARAGE
- DRIVEWAY
- COBBLE EDGE
- FLAGSTONE STEP
- FLAGSTONE WALK
- LAWN EDGING (OPTIONAL)
- 36'-0"
- 120'-0"

The curving borders jut into the lawn, giving it an appealing shape—and a size that isn't too large for the easy-care gardener to handle comfortably. The lawn is kept free of plantings and other obstacles to make mowing faster and easier.

plan# HPT94006

SHOWN IN SPRING
DESIGN BY DAVID POPLAWSKI

SEE PAGE 153 TO ORDER OUR COMPREHENSIVE BLUEPRINT PACKAGE, INCLUDING A REGIONAL-IZED PLANT AND MATERIALS LIST AND OTHER INVALUABLE INFORMATION TO HELP YOU CREATE THIS LANDSCAPE.

COTTAGE GARDEN

Bursting with exuberant old-fashioned blossoms, this friendly cottage garden is designed to be enjoyed from both sides of the fence. The garden invites passersby to pause and enjoy the show from the street or sidewalk, thus creating a friendly neighborhood feeling. However, where space is very limited, you might prefer to plant only the inside of the fence and to plant the street side with a mowing strip of grass or a low-maintenance groundcover. You could even reverse the plan and install the hedge on the street side. Whether you have a sidewalk or not, leave a buffer between the edge of the border and the street so that if you live in a cold-winter climate, there'll be room to pile snow.

Flowering perennial and annual climbing vines cover the wooden arbor, creating a romantic entrance. Roses, bulbs, perennials, annuals, and a compact evergreen hedge are arranged in a classic cottage-garden style that is casual but not haphazard. The designer achieves a pleasant sense of unity by repeating plants and colors throughout the design without repeating a symmetrical planting pattern. This helps create the casual feeling essential to a cottage garden.

Plan View

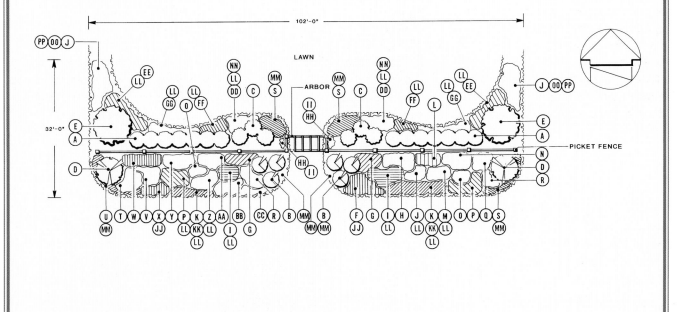

Create a friendly
neighborhood feeling by
planting this flower-filled
cottage garden along the
front of your property.

CHAPTER 3

In Bloom
Flower Gardens

A beautiful flower garden—with its captivating colors and enchanting fragrances—does more than define your yard. It brings your entire home to life, with the promise of gorgeous views in the backyard and cut flowers in every room.

Bright, blooming flowers are the most striking piece of any successful flower garden. But landscape architects will tell you—and the designs in this chapter demonstrate—that it takes more than pretty colors to make your flower garden a success.

We can help you pick the flowers—each plan comes with a regionalized plant list—but here's a quick look at some of the other elements you'll find in the flower gardens in this chapter.

STRUCTURAL ELEMENTS

A garden that focuses primarily on flowers needs some structure so that it looks good all the time. Many of the designs in this chapter use either hardscape structures—such as walls, fences, stepping stones, and arbors—or woody plants to create a sense of permanence and year-round structure that flowers alone can't provide.

During the growing season, structural hardscape elements take a secondary role in a flower garden. In the colder months, when the leaves and flowers are gone, the

RIGHT: Hardscape structures—such as walls, fences, stepping stones, and arbors—create a sense of permanence and year-round structure that flowers alone can't provide.

Comprehensive blueprint packages are available for each of the designs in this chapter. Professionally designed and prepared with precise attention to detail, these easy-to-follow plans include:
- a precise plot plan
- regionalized plant and materials lists
- a plant size and description guide
- installation and maintenance information

These plans will help you or your contractor achieve professional results, adding beauty and value to your property for years. Turn to page 153 for ordering information.

ABOVE: Combine perennials that bloom at the same time for a big impact.

structural elements of a design are more exposed and therefore more dominant, so it's important to consider their individual visual impact. For example, a ramshackle garden shed may look wonderfully charming when it's covered by the blossoms of a rose. However, it may look shabby in the winter, when the stems of the rose are completely bare. The arbor, stone bench, and sculpture in our Romantic Roses plan (page 36) show how the right elements can keep your design looking good year-round.

HEDGES

A sheared evergreen hedge—whether it's very tall or very low—is a traditional way to create a permanent framework for a garden. Yew, boxwood, and Japanese holly are common choices. For a more casual effect, prune the hedge naturally instead of shearing it. You might even wish to add a few compact evergreens to the main garden and allow them to assume their natural, unpruned shape to add year-round greenery.

The hedge at the back of our Blooming Border plan (page 42) is a perfect example of how you can frame your flower garden.

GRASSES

Tall ornamental grasses, added here and there in a garden bed, also make effective structural elements. Although they are

YEARS OF COLOR

When you order blueprints for the landscape designs in this book, you'll receive a regionalized plant list that highlights flowers selected especially for your area. This will give you an easy-to-follow plant list to take to your local nursery, featuring selections that they are likely to have in stock and should be successful in your climate. In the meantime, we have some examples of perennials that can help shape your garden. Narrow your selections based on size and texture, then pick the colors, shapes, and styles of perennials that will suit you—and your garden. Your local nursery may have other suggestions that you'll like as well.

SMALL, DELICATE PERENNIALS

These plants create a cloudlike effect with their fine-textured foliage or their diminutive, delicate flowers that seem to float above the ground. Punctuate drifts of these airy perennials with more substantial plants to provide structure and anchor the design.

    Anemone (*Anemone sylvestris*)
    Astilbe (*Astilbe x hybrida*)
    Baby's breath (*Gypsophila paniculata*)
    Coreopsis (*Coreopsis verticillata 'Moonbeam'*)
    Fennel (*Foeniculum vulgare 'Purpureum'*)
    Forget-me-not (*Myosotis sylvatica*)
    Fringed bleeding heart (*Dicentra eximia*)
    Lavender mist (*Thalictrum rochebrunianum*)
    Perennial flax (*Linum perenne*)
    White gaura (*Gaura lindheimeri*)
    Yellow corydalis (*Corydalis lutea*)

BIG, BOLD PERENNIALS

These perennials are characterized by their boldness—in the size and texture of the leaves, the soaring height of the flower stalks, the striking flowers, or a combination of these traits. Use these sparingly, for drama.

    Agave (*Agave parryi*)
    Cardoon (*Cynara cardunculus*)
    Giant hyssop (*Agastache foeniculum*)
    Giant ornamental onion (*Allium giganteum*)
    Joe-Pye weed (*Eupatorium fistulosum*)
    Red hot poker (*Kniphofia uvaria*)
    Shining coneflower (*Rudbeckia nitida*)
    Spiny bear's breeches (*Acanthus mollis*)
    Yucca (*Yucca filamentosa*)

SPIRELIKE PERENNIALS

Use these and other tall perennials where you want to add a vertical element to a design. Contrast them with mounded or rounded plants.

    Cardinal flower (*Lobelia cardinalis*)
    Delphinium (*Delphinium hybrids*)
    Foxglove (*Digitalis purpurea*)
    Hybrid sage (*Salvia x superba*)
    Lupine (*Lupinus hybrids*)
    Monkshood (*Aconitum spp.*)
    Mullein (*Verbascum x hybridum*)
    Russian sage (*Perovskia atriplicifolia*)
    Veronica (*Veronica spicata*)

herbaceous plants that die back into the ground, their dried foliage and light-catching seed heads stand throughout the winter, adding a pretty note and a lot of volume to the winter garden. Tall grasses also add height to a garden of shorter perennials.

TREES

Small ornamental trees such as magnolia, dogwood, and crabapple not only bring a dramatic spring floral show and fall foliage color to a garden, but also add height, contributing to a three-dimensional effect. Our Easy-Care Beauty plan (page 38) illustrates how trees can add a sense of balance and height to a design, without requiring much maintenance.

Trees cast a bit of shade beneath their boughs, creating a place to grow favorite shade-loving perennials. Deciduous shrubs have the same effect, though on a smaller scale.

PLANTING FLOWERS FOR VISUAL IMPACT

A single plant or flower can easily get lost in a landscape, whereas a large grouping, or mass planting, catches the eye from a distance and draws your interest by its color or form. This is especially true with garden flowers, and large drifts are a technique you'll see repeated in this chapter. In the English Garden, for example (page 40), mass groupings of colorful flowers and the stone path to the garden bench work together to lure you in for a closer look.

Select flower colors that complement other landscape features and any woody plants that bloom at the same time. For example, a large expanse of late pink "Maytime" tulips on one side of a landscape would complement a grouping of pink flowering weigela on the other side. By spreading these drifts apart, it carries the color throughout the landscape. ■

BELOW: By repeating flower drifts, color is carried throughout the landscape.

ROMANTIC ROSES

plan # HPT94008

SHOWN IN SUMMER
DESIGN BY MARIA MORRISON

SEE PAGE 153 TO ORDER OUR COMPREHENSIVE BLUEPRINT PACKAGE, INCLUDING A REGIONALIZED PLANT AND MATERIALS LIST AND OTHER INVALUABLE INFORMATION TO HELP YOU CREATE THIS LANDSCAPE.

Designed to beautify the corner of a backyard, this rose-filled border can be easily turned into a free standing bed and placed in the center of a lawn by rounding off the straight sides into a more free-flowing shape.

Plan View

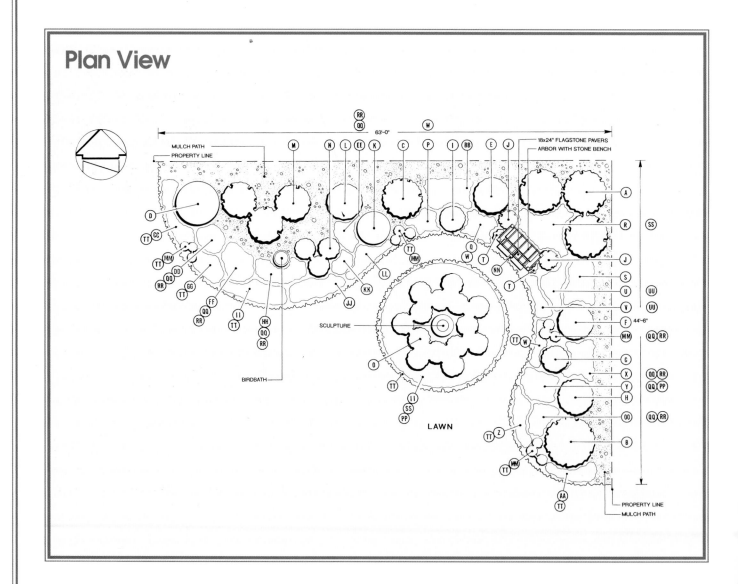

A romantic old-fashioned rose border is always in style. The voluptuous fragrance and heavy-petaled blossoms of roses bring charm to any sunny garden. Here, the designer chooses old garden roses, which offer scent as well as ease of care, unlike modern hybrid tea roses. Although many of these cherished plants bloom only once during the season, their other charms far outweigh the repeat-blossoms of their modern cousins. Many have excellent summer and fall foliage and a heavy crop of glossy rose hips in autumn.

In this border design, these belles of the garden are mixed with classic perennial partners and bulbs to create months of color and interest. A circular bed is tucked into this pleasingly curved border and is separated by a ribbon-like strip of lawn. A rose-covered pergola in the border frames a classically inspired sculpture in the bed's center, creating two balanced focal points. A stone bench placed under the arbor provides a lovely spot to contemplate the wonders of this flower-filled haven. Mulched pathways at the back of the border allow easy access for maintenance and for cutting flowers.

EASY-CARE BEAUTY

plan# HPT94009

SHOWN IN SPRING
DESIGN BY JIM MORGAN

SEE PAGE 153 TO ORDER OUR
COMPREHENSIVE BLUEPRINT
PACKAGE, INCLUDING A REGIONAL-
IZED PLANT AND MATERIALS LIST AND
OTHER INVALUABLE INFORMATION TO
HELP YOU CREATE THIS LANDSCAPE.

Evergreen and deciduous
shrubs and small trees,
mixed with drifts of bulbs
and flowering perennials,
create an ever-changing
border that's gorgeous every
month of the year.

Plan View

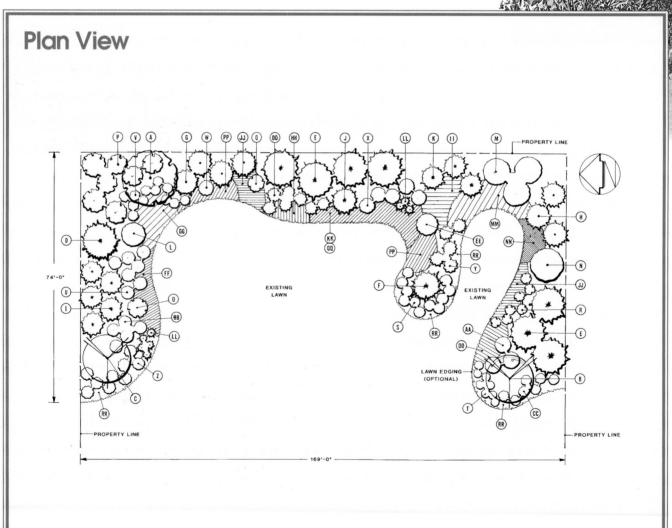

When small trees, flowering shrubs, perennials, and groundcovers are planted together, the result is a lovely mixed border that looks great throughout the year. The trees and shrubs—both evergreen and deciduous types—provide structure and form in winter, while also offering decorative foliage and flowers in other seasons. Perennials and bulbs occupy large spaces between groups of woody plants and contribute leaf texture and floral color to the scene.

Even though this border contains a lot of plants, it is easy to care for. That's part of the beauty of a mixed border—the woody plants are long-lived and need little pruning if allowed to grow naturally. By limiting the number of perennials and blanketing the ground with weed-smothering groundcovers, maintenance is kept to a minimum without sacrificing beauty.

You can install this mixed border in a sunny location almost anywhere on your property, though it's intended to run along the back of an average-sized lot. If your property is larger or smaller than the one in this plan, you can alter the design by either increasing or decreasing the number of plants in each grouping.

ENGLISH GARDEN

A flower-filled garden created in the romantic style of an English border need not demand much care, as this lovely design illustrates. The designer carefully selects unfussy bulbs and perennials and a few flowering shrubs, all of which are disease- and insect-resistant and noninvasive, and don't need staking or other maintenance. A balance of spring-, summer-, and fall-blooming plants keeps the border exciting throughout the growing season. Because English gardens are famous for their gorgeous roses, the designer includes several rosebushes, but chooses ones unharmed by bugs and mildew.

Hedges form a backdrop for most English flower gardens; the designer plants an informal one here to reduce pruning. A generous mulched path runs between the flowers and the hedge, so it's easy to tend them, while the edging keeps grass from invading and creating a nuisance. Plant this border along any sunny side of your property. Imagine it along the back of the yard, where you can view it from a kitchen window or from a patio or deck, along one side of the front yard, or planted with the hedge bordering the front lawn and providing privacy from the street.

Plan View

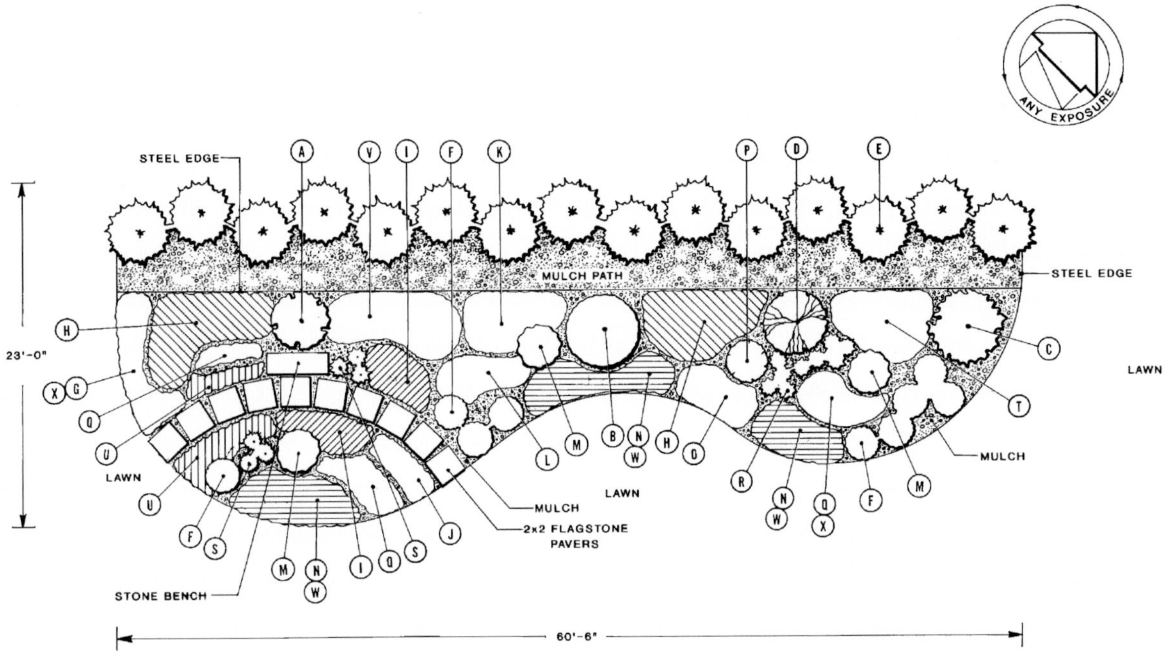

STEEL EDGE

Ⓐ Ⓥ Ⓘ Ⓕ Ⓚ   Ⓟ Ⓓ   Ⓔ

23'-0"

MULCH PATH

STEEL EDGE

Ⓗ

LAWN

Ⓒ

ⓍⒼ

Ⓣ

Ⓠ

LAWN

Ⓤ

Ⓛ Ⓜ Ⓑ Ⓗ
    Ⓝ Ⓖ
    Ⓦ

MULCH

Ⓤ

LAWN

Ⓡ

Ⓝ Ⓠ Ⓕ Ⓜ
Ⓦ   Ⓧ

Ⓕ Ⓢ

Ⓜ Ⓝ Ⓘ Ⓠ Ⓢ
  Ⓦ

Ⓙ

MULCH

2x2 FLAGSTONE
PAVERS

STONE BENCH

|— 60'-6" —|

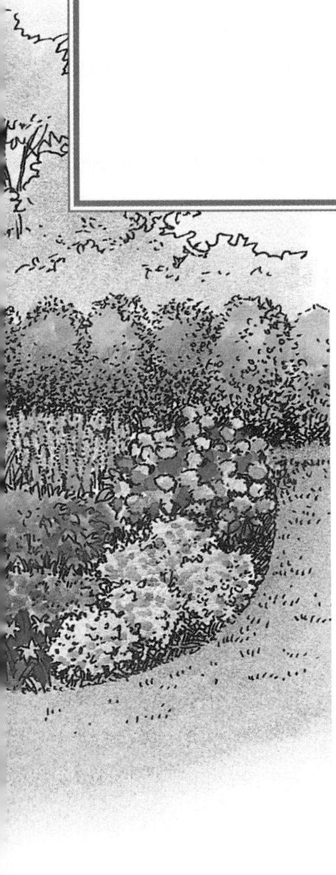

ANY EXPOSURE

Brimming with easy-care flowers from spring through fall, this low-maintenance flower border evokes the spirit of an English garden, but doesn't require a staff to take care of it.

plan ⊕# HPT94010

SHOWN IN SUMMER
DESIGN BY MARIA MORRISON

SEE PAGE 153 TO ORDER OUR COMPREHENSIVE BLUEPRINT PACKAGE, INCLUDING A REGIONALIZED PLANT AND MATERIALS LIST AND OTHER INVALUABLE INFORMATION TO HELP YOU CREATE THIS LANDSCAPE.

BLOOMING BORDER

plan# **HPT94011**

This bed brims with flower color from spring through fall, so be sure to site it in a sunny location where you can enjoy the scene from both indoors and out.

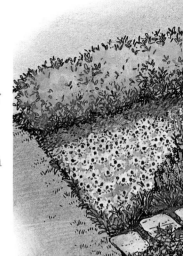

Plan View

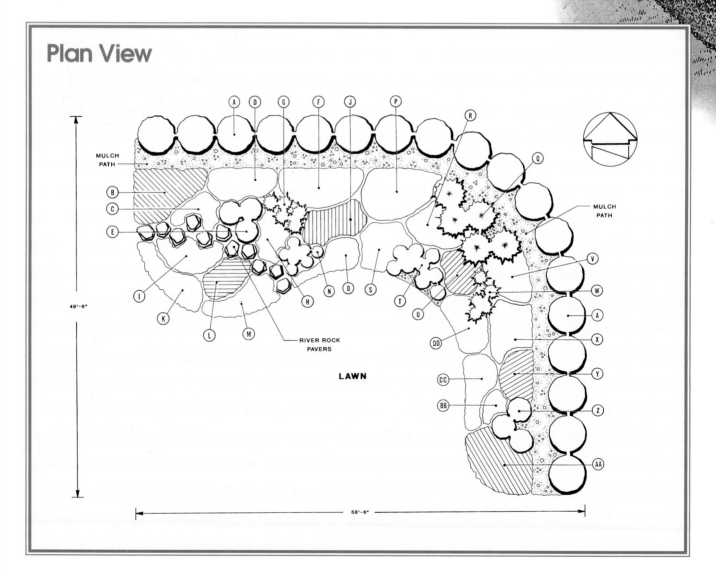

- MULCH PATH
- MULCH PATH
- 49'-6"
- 58'-6"
- RIVER ROCK PAVERS
- LAWN

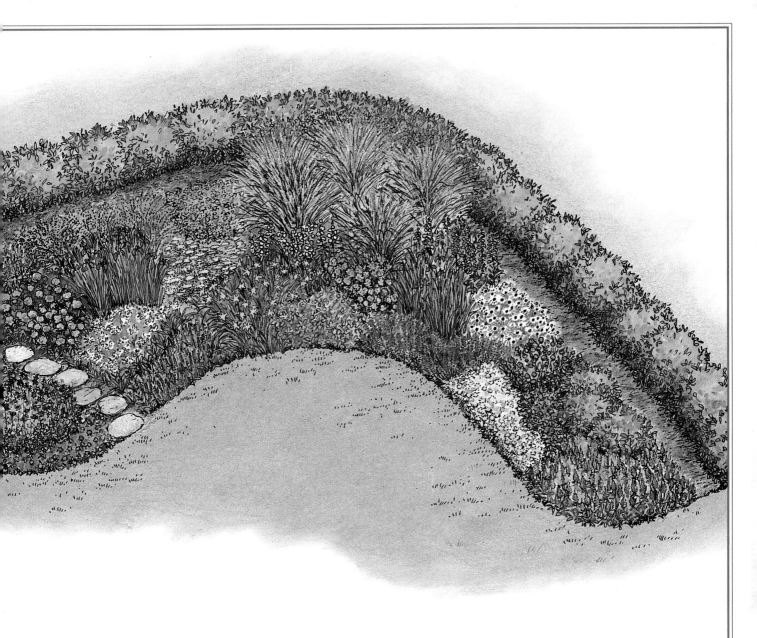

If you'd like to have an easy-care garden that offers more than a single burst of brilliant color, this season-spanning border packed with perennials is perfect for you. The designer selects a wide array of perennials that begin flowering in the spring, provide plenty of color throughout the summer, and continue blooming into the fall. All you'll need to do is remove spent blossoms from time to time and divide plants every few years.

A deciduous hedge curves around the back of the border, providing a pleasant foil for the perennials throughout the growing season. Before dropping its leaves in autumn, the hedge puts on its own show of dazzling color just as the perennials are beginning to slow down. Once the perennials have finished blooming, you can leave the dried flower heads on the plants to add subtle beauty to the winter landscape.

The classic curved shape of this border will fit easily into a corner of your front- or backyard. If you have a large yard, you may want to install this border on one side with its mirror image on the other and with a path set between them.

DOWN-TO-EARTH COLOR SCHEME

Blue and yellow flowers planted together reward the gardener with a naturally complementary color scheme that's as bright and pretty as any garden can be. It's hard to err when using these colors, because the pure blues and the lavender blues—whether dark or pastel—look just as pretty with the pale lemon yellows as with bright sulfur yellows and golden yellows. Each combination makes a different statement, some subtle and sweet as with the pastels, and others bold and demanding as with the deep vivid hues. But no combination fails to please.

The designer of this beautiful bed, which can be situated in any sunny spot, effectively orchestrated a sequence of blue-and-yellow-flowering perennials so the garden blooms from spring through fall. The designer not only combined the floral colors beautifully together, but also incorporated various flower shapes and textures so they make a happy opposition. Fluffy, rounded heads of blossoms set off elegant spires, and mounded shapes mask the lanky stems of taller plants. Large, funnel-shaped flowers stand out against masses of tiny, feathery flowers like jewels displayed against a silk dress.

Although the unmistakable color scheme for this garden is blue and yellow, the designer sprinkled in an occasional spot of orange to provide a lovely jolt of brightly contrasting color. A few masses of creamy white flowers frost the garden, easing the stronger colors into a compatible union.

Plan View

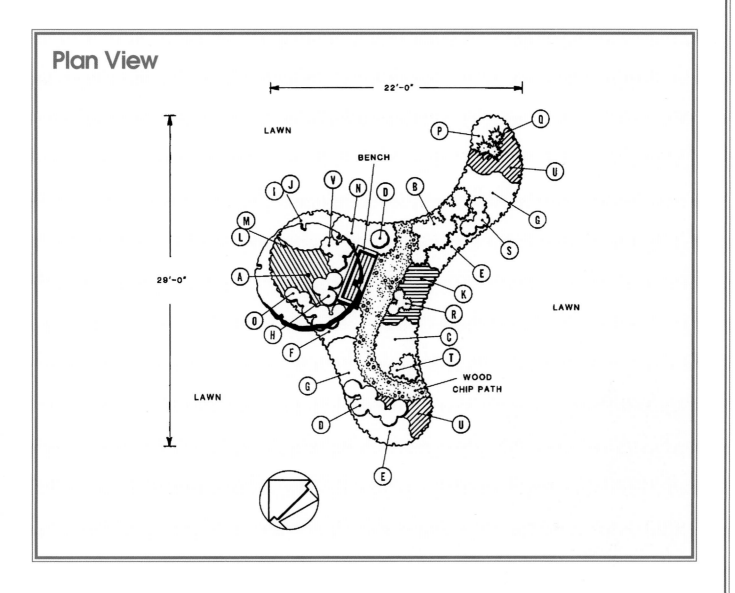

22'-0"

29'-0"

LAWN

BENCH

LAWN

LAWN

WOOD CHIP PATH

plan# **HPT94012**

SHOWN IN SUMMER
DESIGN BY DAMON SCOTT

SEE PAGE 153 TO ORDER OUR COMPREHENSIVE BLUEPRINT PACKAGE, INCLUDING A REGIONALIZED PLANT AND MATERIALS LIST AND OTHER INVALUABLE INFORMATION TO HELP YOU CREATE THIS LANDSCAPE.

Natural color companions, blue and yellow flowers create a pleasing garden scene that looks great anywhere it's planted. This island bed works perfectly in an open sunny yard, but it could be modified to fit along the side of a house or along a property border.

CHAPTER 4

For the Birds
Yards that Attract Wildlife

Homeowners and guests alike can appreciate the sights and smells of a well-planned garden. With the right design, you can also enjoy the added benefits of beautiful butterflies and singing birds.

Birds, butterflies, and other wildlife will flock to your garden and become permanent inhabitants if you provide them with ample food, water, shelter, and nesting sites. Luckily—as the landscapes in this chapter prove—those demands can work hand in hand with a beautiful design.

The easiest and most natural way to supply food is to grow plants that bear seeds and fruits that birds can eat. If you like, you can also set out bird feeders filled with seeds—but with the right design, nature will supply all that your feathered friends need.

Birds tend to visit a garden that offers a source of water even if there isn't much food around. A naturalistic pond, fountain, or stream not only enhances your garden, but also attracts birds and other wildlife if there are shallow areas where they can drink and bathe. A birdbath has a place in a wildlife garden as both a focal point and a wildlife attraction, so don't hesitate to add one if a pond is not in your budget.

RIGHT: This mix of red and pink flowers will help attract hummingbirds, since they associate those colors with food.

Comprehensive blueprint packages are available for each of the designs in this chapter. Professionally designed and prepared with precise attention to detail, these easy-to-follow plans include:
- a precise plot plan
- regionalized plant and materials lists
- a plant size and description guide
- installation and maintenance information

These plans will help you or your contractor achieve professional results, adding beauty and value to your property for years. Turn to page 153 for ordering information.

NATURAL SURROUNDINGS

Birds shy away from birdhouses and feeders set in the middle of a large lawn. Nothing appeals to them there—nothing lures them in, or offers a place to fly for cover. Go beyond the "birdhouse-on-a-bare-pole" look, and add natural elements to make the surroundings more attractive and enticing to birds. For a mounted birdhouse, plant a wide bed of flowers around the post, or stretch your border out to meet the post as seen in our Everything Birds Need plan (page 50). You can also train climbing plants such as small clematis to grow up and around the pole.

If your birdhouse is attached to a tree branch, add a hanging basket of flowers that will rest just beneath it. Birds will be drawn to the flowers, and you'll have double the enjoyment—viewing a scene of colorful flowers as well as flying birds.

When you're landscaping with birds or other wildlife in mind, choose vegetation that offers safety and protection from sun, wind, cold, rain, and predators. Use plants you find attractive that will also provide food and shelter. Birds prefer elderberry and sumac, for example, to forsythia. Use a variety of plants to bring out diverse bird species, and combine low plants and flowers along with tall trees to accommodate ground-dwelling birds as well as those that will seek refuge up high.

ON THE MENU

When it comes to providing birdseed to draw in even more birds, situate the birdfeeder where it's easy to refill. You'll also want to protect the seeds from getting wet and moldy. Sunflower seeds are the favorite of many birds, and when you buy them you get a choice: messy or money. With the unhulled type, birds eat the seeds and spill the outer shells on the ground. Hulled seeds—or sunflower hearts—are neater, since there's no shell to leave on the ground, but they're more expensive.

Other treats for birds include millet, cracked corn, orange slices, and berries. During cold weather, birds need an added source of energy, such as suet. Offer some grit, in the form of large-grain sand or cracked eggshells, and birds will use it to grind their food.

The alternative is to let the birds forage for themselves. Help them out with flowers and shrubs that produce seeds or berries, such as cosmos, flax, sunflowers, purple coneflowers, and bayberry. Decide which birds you want to see, then plant the vegetation they like—chances are there will be a good overlap between the birds that are common in your area and the plants and flowers that will grow well there. Of course, birds eat insects as well. If your flowers attract outdoor pests, hungry birds will help you get rid of them.

The last item on the menu is beverage, something that each of the five designs in this chapter offers (as do the designs in Chapter 7, Private Oasis). Include a pond, birdbath, or even a hidden pan of water to quench their thirst, and if you need to, replenish it every few days.

Besides beverage, water serves another purpose: cleanliness. In the winter, especially, birds use water to keep their feathers clean so that they will provide better insulation. You'll quickly find that all year-round, nothing quite beats watching the birds flock to your garden to splash around in the bath. ■

LEFT: Adding water to any landscape— whether it's a pond, waterfall, or just a birdbath—will help attract wildlife.

ATTRACTING HUMMINGBIRDS OR BUTTERFLIES

There are very specific requirements when you are trying to attract hummingbirds and butterflies, two species that are big favorites among gardeners.

Hummingbirds associate red with food, and will investigate anything that color—whether it's a red flower or a red bandanna hanging on the clothesline to dry. The best flowers for attracting hummingbirds are pink, red, or orange nectar-bearing blossoms with a tubular shape to accommodate their long beaks.

Hummingbirds are very territorial and will do their utmost to keep others out of their feeding area. Not only will a hummingbird challenge other hummers, it may even try to chase off butterflies, other small birds, and even small animals such as chipmunks with loud noises and a fluttering of wings. Because they're so territorial, you may need to create separate plantings throughout your yard in order to attract more than one hummingbird pair.

When gardening for butterflies, most people tend to forget the less attractive—and sometimes destructive—caterpillar stage. Instead of spurning all caterpillars in the garden, you need to differentiate between "good bugs" and "bad bugs" in order to enjoy an abundance of butterflies. Knowing that the caterpillar eating its way through the foliage of your parsley, dill, and carrots will grow to become a gorgeous black swallowtail butterfly helps you to look more favorably on it. Try to plant enough parsley to feed yourself and the caterpillars so that later you can enjoy both herbs and butterflies.

You'll also want to learn which butterflies are native to your locale and identify them in the caterpillar stage. That way you can still pick off destructive caterpillars, such as the tomato hornworm and the cabbage white butterfly, while nurturing those that will later spin cocoons and hatch into charming butterflies.

EVERYTHING BIRDS NEED

This border includes everything birds need—food, water, and nesting sites—and encourages them to become permanent residents of your yard. The design curves inward, creating a sense of enclosure and a sanctuary that appeals to even the shiest types of birds. The border's attractive design includes a pond, birdhouse, and birdbath, which act as focal points and make the garden irresistible to people as well.

The large variety of pretty fruiting shrubs offers birds natural nourishment throughout much of the year, but you can supplement the food supply with store-bought bird food if you wish. Deciduous and evergreen trees provide shelter and nesting places, while the mulched areas give birds a place to take dust baths and to poke around for insects and worms.

Because water is so important to birds, the garden includes two water features: a small naturalistic pond and a birdbath set in a circular bed. Both offer spots for perching, bathing, and drinking. In cold-weather climates, consider adding a special heater the birdbath to keep the water from freezing; water attracts birds in winter even more than birdseed.

Plan View

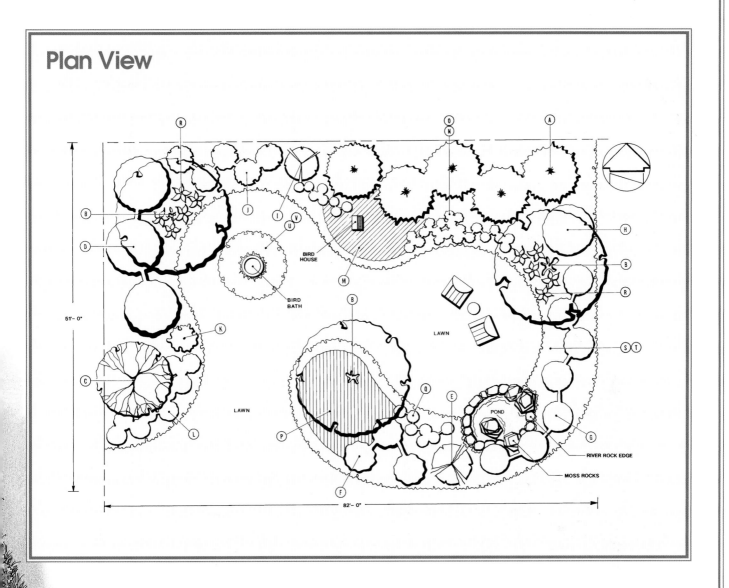

BIRD
HOUSE

BIRD
BATH

LAWN

LAWN

POND

RIVER ROCK EDGE

MOSS ROCKS

51'– 0"

82'– 0"

Birds flock to this border, which provides them with ample supplies of food and water and locations for nesting and bathing. There's plenty of room for bird-watchers as well.

plan ⊕ HPT94013

SHOWN IN SUMMER
DESIGN BY MICHAEL J. OPISSO

SEE PAGE 153 TO ORDER OUR COMPREHENSIVE BLUEPRINT PACKAGE, INCLUDING A REGIONALIZED PLANT AND MATERIALS LIST AND OTHER INVALUABLE INFORMATION TO HELP YOU CREATE THIS LANDSCAPE.

BIRDWATCHING FROM THE DECK

plan# HPT94014

SHOWN IN AUTUMN
DESIGN BY MICHAEL J. OPISSO

SEE PAGE 153 TO ORDER OUR COMPREHENSIVE BLUEPRINT PACKAGE, INCLUDING A REGIONALIZED PLANT AND MATERIALS LIST AND OTHER INVALUABLE INFORMATION TO HELP YOU CREATE THIS LANDSCAPE.

Nature lovers will delight in the abundant number of birds that will flock to this beautiful garden. An attractive collection of berried plants and evergreens offers food and shelter for the wildlife, while creating a handsome, pastoral setting.

Plan View

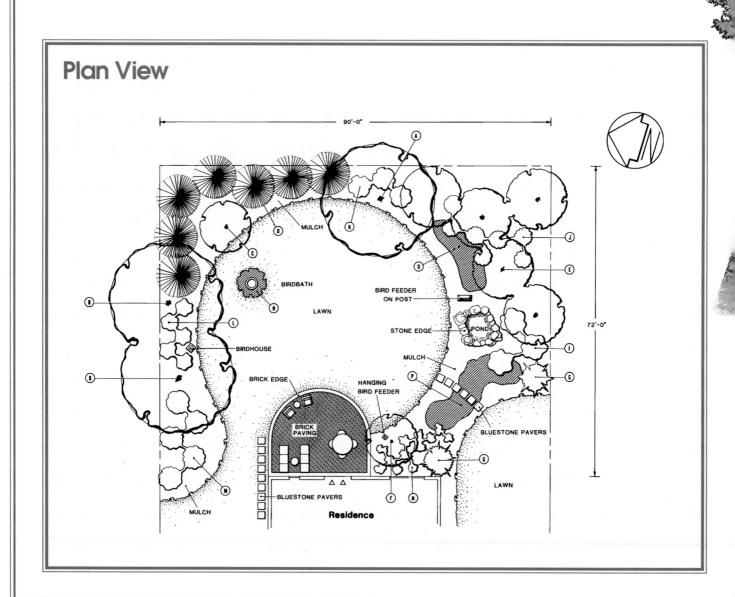

There is no better way to wake up in the morning than to the sound of songbirds in the garden. Wherever you live, you will be surprised at the number and variety of birds you can attract by offering them a few basic necessities—water, shelter, nesting spots, and food. Birds need water for drinking and bathing. They need shrubs and trees, especially evergreens, for shelter and nesting. Edge spaces—open areas with trees nearby for quick protection—provide ground feeders with foraging places, while plants with berries and nuts offer other natural sources of food.

The garden presented here contains all the necessary elements to attract birds to the garden. The shrubs and trees are chosen especially to provide a mix of evergreen and deciduous species. All of these, together with the masses of flowering perennials,

bear seeds, nuts, or berries that are known to appeal to birds. The berry show looks quite pretty, too, until the birds gobble them up! Planted densely enough for necessary shelter, the bird-attracting plants create a lovely private backyard that's enjoyable throughout the seasons.

The birdbath is located in the lawn so it will be in the sun. A naturalistic pond provides water in a more protected setting. The birdhouses and feeders aren't really necessary—though they may be the icing on the cake when it comes to luring the largest number of birds—because the landscape provides abundant natural food and shelter. Outside one of the main windows of the house, a birdfeeder hangs from a small flowering tree, providing an up-close view of your feathered friends.

SONGBIRD GARDEN

This naturalistic garden plan relies upon several different features to attract as many different species of birds as possible. A songbird's basic needs include food, water, and shelter, but this backyard plan offers luxury accommodations not found in every yard, and also provides the maximum opportunity for birds and bird-watchers to observe each other. Special features provide for specific birds; for example, the weathered log attracts woodpeckers and the dusting area will be used gratefully by birds to free themselves of parasites. In addition to plants that produce plentiful berries and seeds, the designer includes a ground feeder to lure morning doves, cardinals, and other birds that prefer to eat off the ground. The birdhouse located in the shade of the specimen tree to the rear of the garden suits a wide variety of songbirds.

The angular deck nestles attractively into the restful circular shapes of the garden. The designer encloses the deck amidst the bird-attracting plantings to maximize close-up observation opportunities and create an intimate setting. Two other sitting areas welcome bird-watchers into the garden. A bench positioned on a small patio under the shade of a graceful flowering tree provides a relaxing spot to sit and contemplate the small garden pool and the melody of a low waterfall. Another bench—this one situated in the sun—may be reached by strolling along a path of wood-rounds on the opposite side of the yard. Both wildlife and people will find this backyard a very special retreat.

ORDER BLUEPRINTS 24 HOURS, 7 DAYS A WEEK, AT 1-800-521-6797

Plan View

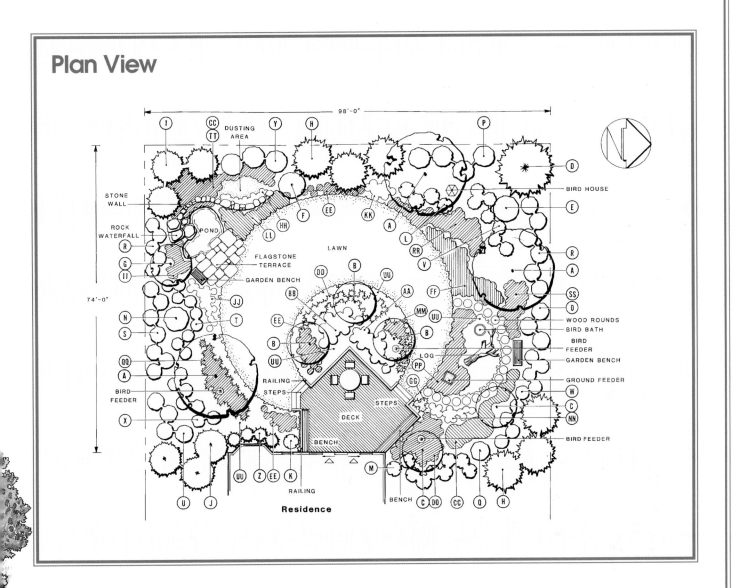

This large, naturalistic backyard design creates a wonderful environment for attracting a wide range of bird species, because it offers a plentiful supply of natural food, water, and shelter. The deck and garden benches invite people to observe and listen to the songbirds in comfort.

plan #️ HPT94015

SHOWN IN SPRING
DESIGN BY DAVID POPLAWSKI

SEE PAGE 153 TO ORDER OUR COMPREHENSIVE BLUEPRINT PACKAGE, INCLUDING A REGIONAL-IZED PLANT AND MATERIALS LIST AND OTHER INVALUABLE INFORMATION TO HELP YOU CREATE THIS LANDSCAPE.

SPLASH IN THE BIRDBATH

plan# HPT94016

SHOWN IN SUMMER
DESIGN BY PATRICK J. DUFFE

SEE PAGE 153 TO ORDER OUR
COMPREHENSIVE BLUEPRINT
PACKAGE, INCLUDING A REGIONAL-
IZED PLANT AND MATERIALS LIST AND
OTHER INVALUABLE INFORMATION TO
HELP YOU CREATE THIS LANDSCAPE.

Sit beneath the flower-draped
pergola and enjoy glimpses of
hummingbirds as they pause in
midflight to drink nectar and
splash in the birdbath.

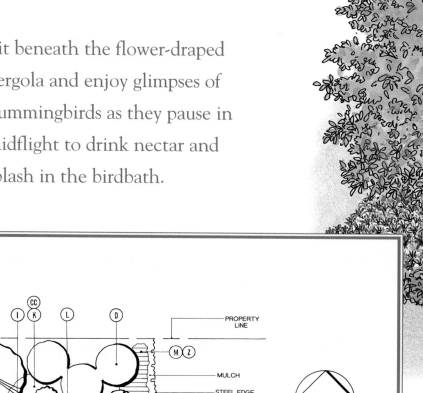

Plan View

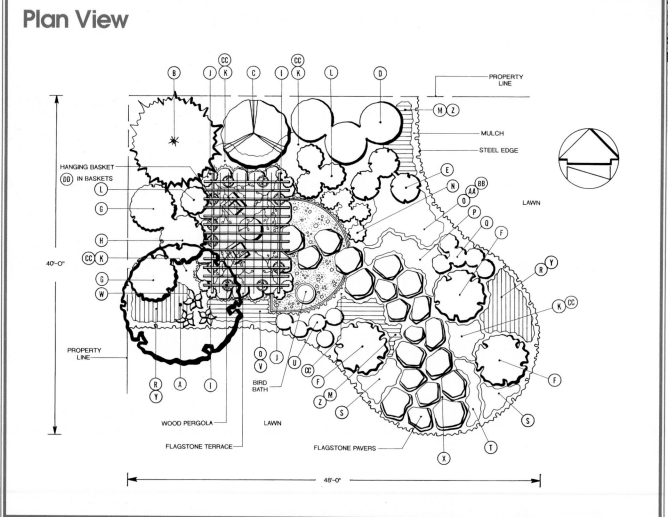

Your yard will be home to jewel-toned, quicksilver hummingbirds once you install this colorful bed. A rich display of bright annuals and perennials, specially selected to attract hummingbirds, creates a delightful setting. All birds need water, and because hummingbirds are particularly attracted to flowing water, the birdbath in this design features a small bubbler device.

Informal flagstone pavers lead through the garden to a semicircular mulched area set with flagstones that surround the birdbath. The path to the wooden pergola (not included in plans), which cre-

ates a lovely sitting area, leads through the pretty flowers. Climbing vines and hanging planters attached to the pergola provide additional nectar and create a pleasant shady area where you can watch the hummers dart by. Hang the pots so you can watch the birds at eye level from the sitting area. Neutral-colored plastic pots look best and cut down on evaporation, minimizing watering chores.

Site this design in a sunny location close to your house so you can observe the birds from indoors as well. Or, if you prefer, locate the bed in a quiet corner of your yard to enhance the tranquil atmosphere.

WILDLIFE SANCTUARY

plan# **HPT94017**

SHOWN IN AUTUMN
DESIGN BY SALVATORE A. MASULLO

SEE PAGE 153 TO ORDER OUR COMPREHENSIVE BLUEPRINT PACKAGE, INCLUDING A REGIONALIZED PLANT AND MATERIALS LIST AND OTHER INVALUABLE INFORMATION TO HELP YOU CREATE THIS LANDSCAPE.

Filled with fruiting shrubs, trees, ornamental grasses, and perennials that provide food for birds, this border is as beautiful as it is bird friendly.

Plan View

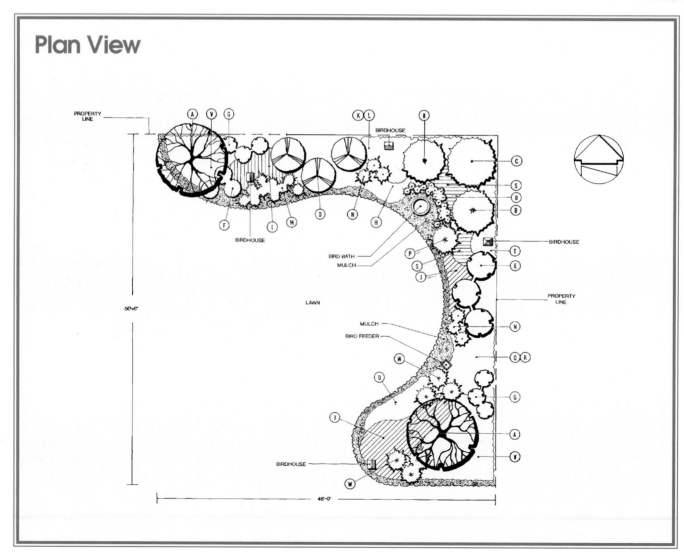

This attractive border does double duty, because it serves both as a beautiful landscape planting as well as an effective wildlife sanctuary. Offering natural food sources, shelter, and water, the planting brings birds to your property throughout the year, while its informal but tidy design looks right at home in any suburban setting. Although they serve a practical purpose as well, the birdhouses, bird feeders, and birdbath add interesting architectural elements to the design.

The shrubs and trees used in the border—and even many of the perennials and ornamental grasses—produce berries and seeds that attract birds. They are arranged informally and should be left unpruned to form a dense shelter for nesting sites. Because most berried plants produce best when cross-pollinated by another similar plant, the designer masses specimens together and repeats plants.

You can site this border along the property lines in either your front- or backyard, or round off its corners and use it as an island planting. Then sit back and enjoy the birds and birdsongs that fill your garden.

CHAPTER 5

Take it Easy
Low-Maintenance Landscaping

Gardens can be inspiring without being back-breaking—you must, as they say, stop and smell the roses, not spend all your time caring for them. Choose a design featuring plants that flourish with minimal attention, and you can enjoy a lovely garden without all the work.

A gardener once said that the only maintenance-free lawn he ever saw was a stretch of solid concrete painted green. No maintenance, perhaps, but not particularly attractive either.

The definition of low-maintenance is certainly subjective—someone who hates to work outdoors may consider a yard that needs one hour of attention each week low maintenance, whereas an avid gardener may consider six hours a week easy to care for. Only you know how much time you wish to devote to caring for your yard and garden.

The easy-care plans featured in this section are a far cry from green concrete, yet they don't take much care on a weekly or even monthly basis. The designers consid-

ered the maintenance needs of the yards when creating these designs, making conscious choices to reduce the work involved in keeping the yards healthy and attractive. Here are some of the time-saving principles you'll see put to use in this chapter:

■ Reduce the size of the lawn; replace turf with ground covers, hardscape, or mulched shrub borders.

■ Apply organic mulch, such as wood chips, under permanent plantings to reduce the need to water and weed.

■ Plant dwarf or slow-growing varieties of

RIGHT: Ornamental grasses mixed with flowering plants can provide a beautiful and efficient border in an easy-care landscape.

Comprehensive blueprint packages are available for each of the designs in this chapter. Professionally designed and prepared with precise attention to detail, these easy-to-follow plans include:
  ■ a precise plot plan
  ■ regionalized plant and materials lists
  ■ a plant size and description guide
  ■ installation and maintenance information
These plans will help you or your contractor achieve professional results, adding beauty and value to your property for years. Turn to page 153 for ordering information.

shrubs that won't need routine pruning to keep them under control.

■ Choose trees with compound leaves made up of tiny leaflets to make fall raking an easy chore.

■ Underplant trees with ground covers that absorb fallen leaves and debris to reduce cleanup.

■ Install weed barriers beneath gravel, paving, or mulch to prevent weeds.

■ Keep unconnected lawn areas and specimen plantings in the lawn to a minimum to ease mowing chores.

■ Install permanent borders or edgings between the lawn and planting beds to eliminate the need to trim lawn edges and to keep grass out of shrubs and flower beds.

■ Choose easy-care perennials and flowering shrubs rather than high-maintenance annuals for floral beauty.

■ Choose disease-resistant, well-adapted plants that don't need constant pest-proofing, watering, pruning, staking, or other pampering to thrive.

Just because it's easy to care for doesn't mean your backyard can't be beautiful, as the five plans in this chapter demonstrate. By employing some or all of these techniques, the landscapes presented here will require less time on labor—giving you more time to enjoy their beauty.

A LOVELY YARD WITH LESS LAWN

A lawn is the biggest thief of time in any garden. It seemingly requires constant attention: No sooner have you turned your back than the grass needs another mowing, liming, or fertilizing—or it's been invaded by grubs or a fungus.

You can still create that cool greenbelt feeling in your backyard by reducing the lawn to a more manageable size. Lawns of 3,000 to 5,000 square feet are large enough to look nice while being small enough to be easily cared for. You might also consider

planting a low-maintenance grass variety—one that grows slowly and resists drought.

By installing a steel or vinyl lawn edging or a brick mowing strip between the lawn and garden beds, you can keep the two areas separate. The lawn will stay on its side of the border and creeping ground covers on their side. This translates into less weeding, and a neater look without the time-consuming chore of edging the lawn. When properly installed so the lawn mower wheels glide right over the edging or mowing strip, you won't have to go back with a hand clipper or string-trimmer to cut scraggly edges.

OTHER ALTERNATIVES TO GRASS

Alternatives to lawn grass—like evergreen plants such as periwinkle (myrtle), English ivy, mondograss, pachysandra, wintercreeper, and prostrate juniper—can provide a low-maintenance ground cover. Plant these in large swatches around the borders of a greatly reduced lawn, or replace the lawn entirely with ground cover. If you need access to a patio, gate, or garden, provide stepping stones as a path through the planting.

Replacing all or part of a lawn with gravel, stones, or sand creates a naturalistic look, and is another alternative to grass. You can find different sizes of gravel or stone, but keep in mind that small stones are easier to walk on and dark colors generally look better than light ones. Be sure to use landscape fabric, or geotextile, under the stones or sand to prevent weeds from growing up from the soil while allowing water to drain through to tree and shrub roots underneath.

Another substitute for grass is a meadow garden. Highly adaptable, these ornamental grasses grow in almost any type of soil and are attractive throughout the year. In the spring, they quickly grow to their full height and volume. Their long leaves sway in summer breezes, and, by late summer, the plants send up spikes or plumes of flowers, which form attractive seed heads by fall. As the temperatures drop, their green foliage fades to bright beige, almond, or wheat for the winter. The dried foliage and flowers of

most types remain through the winter, adding height and texture to your yard.

The only maintenance most ornamental grasses require is to be cut to the ground in the spring, just as new growth begins. Dispose of the cuttings by shredding them in a chipper-shredder.

MULCH MAKES A DIFFERENCE

Once you've planted your low-maintenance garden, mulch it well with wood chips, shredded leaves, or another attractive organic material to further reduce the garden chores. The importance of mulching can't be overemphasized. Not only does a 3-inch layer of mulch cut down drastically on weeds, but it also insulates the soil and keeps moisture in so you don't have to water as frequently. While ground covers will eventually blanket the soil and crowd out most weeds, you may still wish to apply an initial layer of mulch to combat weeds until the new planting fills in.

Don't put mulch right up against the stem or trunk of any plant, but rather 1 or 2 inches from the base. When piled right up against a plant, mulch can smother the lower stem or cause it to rot. An organic mulch eventually decays, adding beneficial material and nutrients to the soil, and needs to be refreshed every year or so. Black plastic mulch doesn't let rain into the soil and isn't recommended for use beneath shrubs and trees, although it can be a good choice for vegetable gardens if you have an irrigation system beneath the plastic.

CHOICES, CHOICES

Plant choices are a big part of a low-maintenance landscape. The designers who created the plans in this chapter took care to select plant options that are easy to maintain and resist diseases and insects. Plants that are well-suited to your area will make your gardening life easier as well—when you order blueprints for these plans you'll receive a regionalized plant and materials list to help ensure success in your locale. ■

DROUGHT-TOLERANT GARDEN

plan⊕# HPT94018

SHOWN IN SUMMER
DESIGN BY DAMON SCOTT

SEE PAGE 153 TO ORDER OUR COMPREHENSIVE BLUEPRINT PACKAGE, INCLUDING A REGIONALIZED PLANT AND MATERIALS LIST AND OTHER INVALUABLE INFORMATION TO HELP YOU CREATE THIS LANDSCAPE.

This environmentally sound landscape plan won't strain the local water supply or burden you with gardening chores, because all the plants used here—from grass to flowers to trees—are easy-care, trouble-free kinds that flourish without frequent rain or irrigation.

Plan View

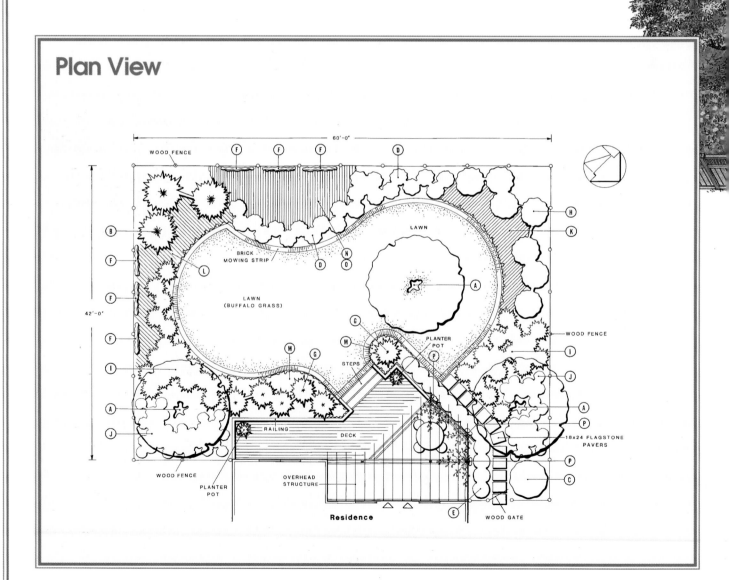

This design proves that "drought tolerant" and "low maintenance" don't have to mean boring. This attractive backyard looks lush, colorful, and inviting, but relies entirely on plants that flourish even if water is scarce. This means you won't spend any time tending to their watering needs once the plantings are established. Even the lawn is planted with a newly developed turf grass that tolerates long periods of drought.

The designer specifies buffalo grass, a native grass of the American West, for the lawn. The grass has fine-textured, grayish-green leaf blades, tolerates cold, and needs far less water to remain green and healthy than most lawns. It goes completely dormant during periods of extended drought, but greens up with rain or irrigation. To keep the lawn green throughout summer, all you need do is water occasionally if rainfall doesn't cooperate. And mowing is an occasional activity, too! This slow-growing grass needs mowing only a few times in summer to about one inch high. To keep the grass from spreading into the planting borders—and to reduce weeding and edging chores—the designer calls for a decorative brick mowing strip surrounding the lawn.

Deciduous and evergreen trees and shrubs interplanted with long-blooming flowering perennials—all drought-tolerant—adorn the yard, bringing color every season. Against the fence grow espaliered shrubs, which offer flowers in spring and berries in winter. The vine-covered trellis shades the roomy, angular deck, where you can sit in cool seclusion and relax while your beautiful backyard takes care of itself.

JAPANESE-STYLE GARDEN

When a busy family wants a landscape that is distinctive and requires little maintenance, the Japanese-style garden and backyard pictured here are a perfect solution. The essence of a Japanese garden lies in emulating nature through simple, clean lines that do not look contrived. The low, tight hedges underscore the plantings behind them, while providing a contrast in form. Looking straight out from the deck, the perimeter planting is a harmony of shades of green, with interest provided from contrasting textures.

Paving stones border the deck because in the Japanese garden, every element has both an aesthetic and a functional purpose. The stones alleviate the wear that would result from stepping directly onto the lawn from the deck, and provide a visual tran-

sition between the man-made deck and the natural grass. The pavers act as more than a path; they also provide a sight line to the stone lantern on the left side of the garden.

The deck, like the rest of the landscape, has clean, simple lines, and provides the transition from the home's interior to the garden. It surrounds a viewing garden, one step down. In the Japanese tradition, this miniature landscape mimics a natural scene. The one large moss rock plays an important role—it is situated at the intersection of the stepping-stone paths that lead through the garden. Here a decision must be made as to which way to turn. The stone water basin, a symbolic part of the Japanese tea ceremony, is located near the door to the house, signaling the entrance to a very special place.

ORDER BLUEPRINTS 24 HOURS, 7 DAYS A WEEK, AT 1-800-521-6797

Plan View

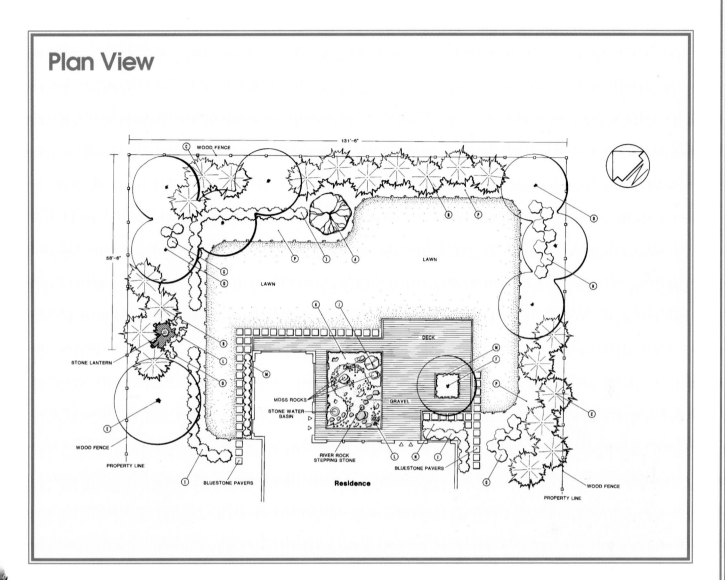

This beautiful Japanese-style garden provides space for outdoor living and entertaining in a tranquil setting. Featuring straight, simple lines, a small lawn, a large deck, and extensive plantings of groundcovers and evergreens, the garden practically cares for itself.

plan# HPT94019

SHOWN IN SPRING
DESIGN BY MICHAEL J. OPISSO

SEE PAGE 153 TO ORDER OUR COMPREHENSIVE BLUEPRINT PACKAGE, INCLUDING A REGIONALIZED PLANT AND MATERIALS LIST AND OTHER INVALUABLE INFORMATION TO HELP YOU CREATE THIS LANDSCAPE.

RAISED FLOWER BED

A colorful, easy-care flower bed like this paisley-shaped raised bed can be located almost anywhere on your property—it is perfectly suitable as an entry garden, or as a transition between different levels in a backyard. The bed's curving, organic shape echoes the sinuous stone wall that divides its upper and lower sections. Flagstone steps further divide the bed and lead visitors from the lower, more symmetrical area to the upper, more asymmetrical section of the garden.

The designer incorporates lovely low-growing flowering perennials to spill over the wall, creating a curtain of flowers. Twin flowering shrubs flank the entry steps, while a single specimen of the same type marks the exit. The rest of the bed is planted with a profusion of easy-care perennials, bulbs, ornamental grasses, and flowering shrubs.

This garden bed requires only a little of your precious time for routine maintenance. You'll need to remove spent blossoms, do a bit of cleanup in spring and fall, and divide the perennials every few years.

Plan View

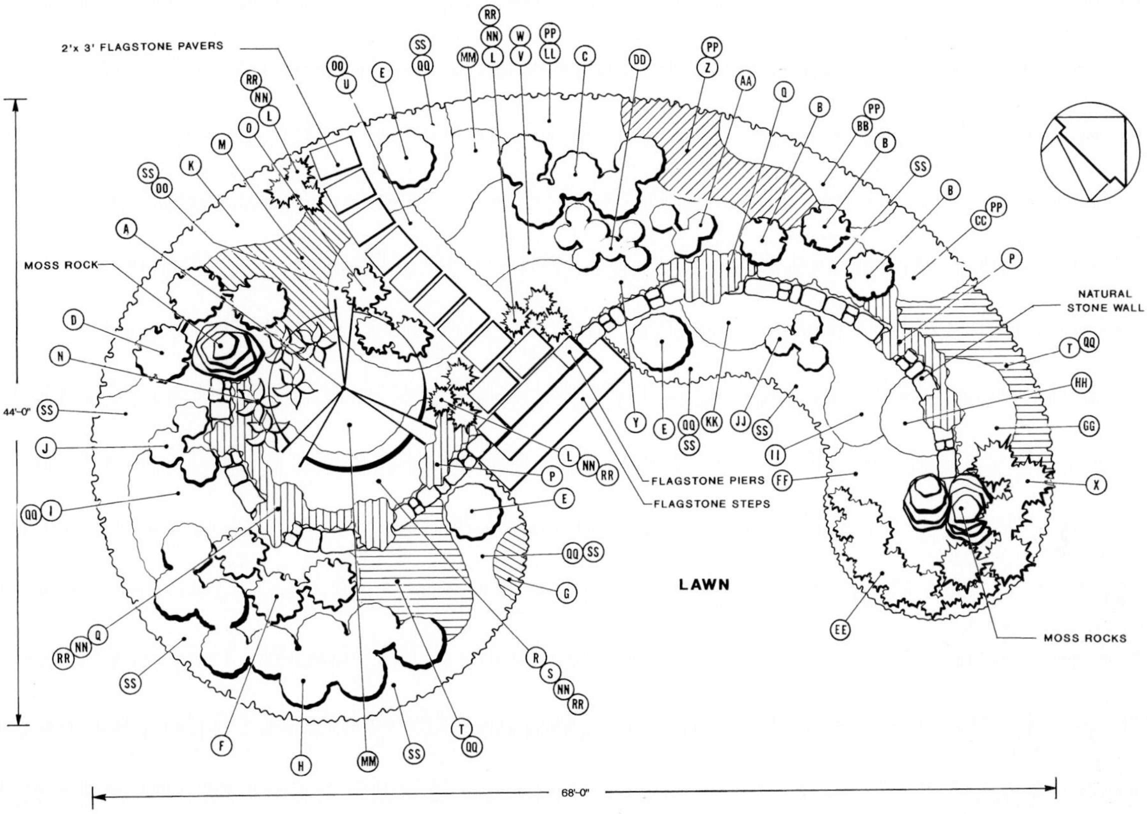
2'x 3' FLAGSTONE PAVERS
MOSS ROCK
NATURAL STONE WALL
FLAGSTONE PIERS
FLAGSTONE STEPS
LAWN
MOSS ROCKS
44'-0"
68'-0"

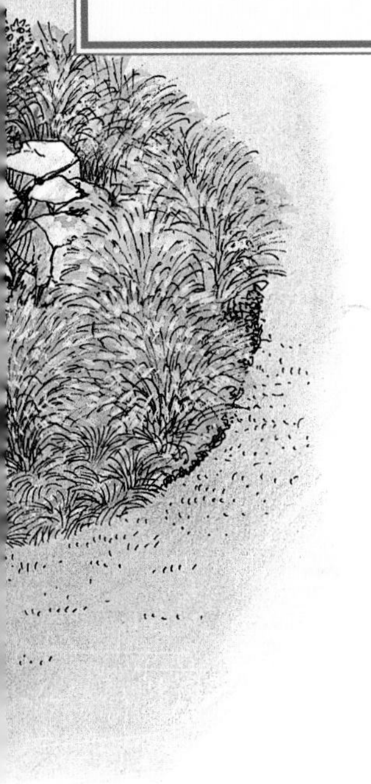

A curving stone retaining wall and small flowering tree give this flower garden dimension and form, which keep it attractive throughout the year.

plan # HPT94020

SHOWN IN SUMMER
DESIGN BY SALVATORE A. MASULLO

SEE PAGE 153 TO ORDER OUR COMPREHENSIVE BLUEPRINT PACKAGE, INCLUDING A REGIONALIZED PLANT AND MATERIALS LIST AND OTHER INVALUABLE INFORMATION TO HELP YOU CREATE THIS LANDSCAPE.

YEAR-ROUND COLOR

One of the great joys of a lovely low-maintenance garden is having the time to really enjoy it. If you'd like a garden bed that is eye-catching as well as easy-care, this design is for you. This bow-tie-shaped bed contains a delightful variety of low-maintenance perennials, evergreens, deciduous trees and shrubs, and spring bulbs. Such a diverse blend of easy-care plants guarantees you'll have both year-round color and the time to take pleasure in every season's display.

The berms at each end of the bed create a small valley that is traversed by a natural stone path. Trees screen the peak of the higher berm, adding a bit of mystery and encouraging visitors to explore. Two pathways—one of mulch, the other of stepping stones—make it easy to enjoy the plantings up close and to perform maintenance tasks, such as occasional deadheading and weeding. Moss rocks in three areas of the garden and a birdhouse near the stepping-stone path provide pleasing structure and interest.

Plan View

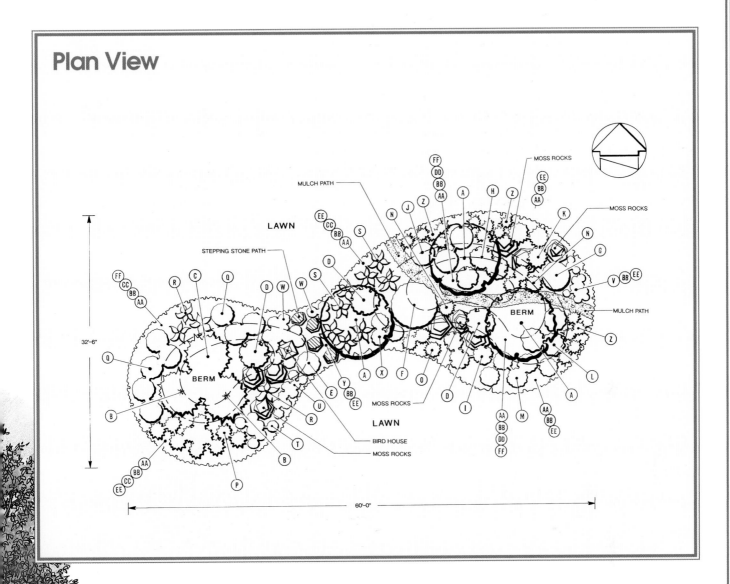

LAWN

MULCH PATH

MOSS ROCKS

MOSS ROCKS

MOSS ROCKS

STEPPING STONE PATH

32'-6"

BERM

BERM

LAWN

BIRD HOUSE

MOSS ROCKS

MULCH PATH

60'-0"

plan # HPT94021

SHOWN IN SUMMER
DESIGN BY JEFFERY DIEFENBACH

SEE PAGE 153 TO ORDER OUR COMPREHENSIVE BLUEPRINT PACKAGE, INCLUDING A REGIONALIZED PLANT AND MATERIALS LIST AND OTHER INVALUABLE INFORMATION TO HELP YOU CREATE THIS LANDSCAPE.

Locate this easy-care bed in an open area of lawn in the front- or backyard to create a pretty view that can be enjoyed from indoors and out.

EASY-CARE SHRUB BORDER

Nothing beats flowering shrubs and trees for an easy-care show of flowers and foliage throughout the seasons. This lovely garden includes shrubs that bloom at various times of the year—from late winter right into autumn—so that blossoms will always be decorating this garden. In autumn, the leaves of the deciduous shrubs turn flaming shades of yellow, gold, orange, and red. (These colors appear even more brilliant when juxtaposed against the deep greens of the evergreen shrubs.) During the coldest months, when the flowers and fall foliage are finally finished, many of the plants feature glossy red berries or evergreen leaves that take on deep burgundy hues.

The designer balances the border with a tall evergreen and two flowering trees, which serve as anchors at the border's widest points. Most shrubs are grouped in all-of-a-kind drifts to create the most impact—low, spreading types in the front and taller ones in the back—but several specimens appear alone as eye-catching focal points. A few large drifts of easy-care, long-blooming perennials, interplanted with spring-flowering bulbs, break up the shrubbery to give a variety of textures and forms.

Designed for the back of an average-sized lot, this easy-care border can be located in any sunny area of your property. It makes a perfect addition to any existing property, adds year-round interest, creates privacy, and reduces maintenance.

ORDER BLUEPRINTS 24 HOURS, 7 DAYS A WEEK, AT 1-800-521-6797

Plan View

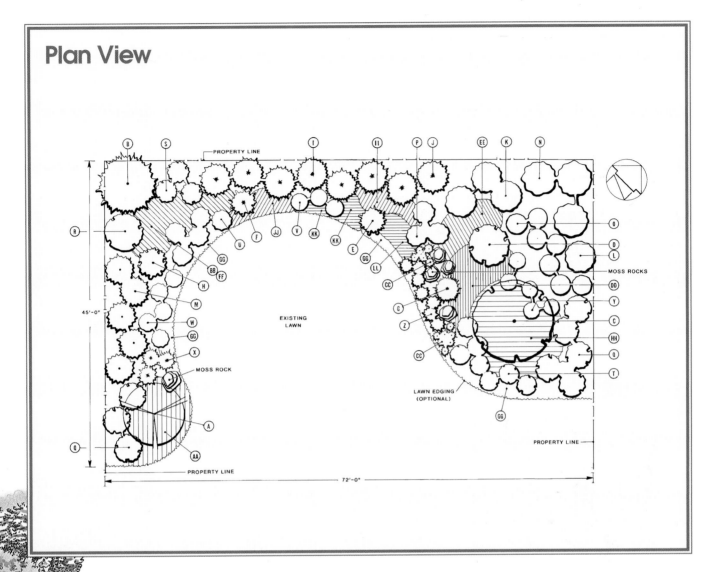

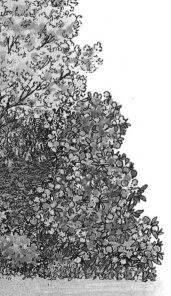

When easy-care, disease- and insect-resistant shrubs are used to create a border, and allowed to grow naturally without excessive pruning, the result is a beautiful, practically maintenance-free garden.

plan # HPT94022

SHOWN IN SPRING
DESIGN BY SALVATORE A. MASULLO

SEE PAGE 153 TO ORDER OUR COMPREHENSIVE BLUEPRINT PACKAGE, INCLUDING A REGIONALIZED PLANT AND MATERIALS LIST AND OTHER INVALUABLE INFORMATION TO HELP YOU CREATE THIS LANDSCAPE.

CHAPTER 6

Seasons in the Shade
Gardens for Shady Sites

A cool, colorful shade garden can be a perfect place to escape during hot, hazy summer days. With an amazing number of shade-loving flowers and plants available, a lack of sunlight won't stop you from creating the landscape of your dreams.

Gardening in less than full sun certainly provides some challenges, but it won't keep you from creating a beautiful yard. In fact, cool, shady gardens offer a tranquil respite from the hot summer sun. The designs showcased in this chapter feature plants that will thrive in shady areas, providing you with beautiful, engaging landscapes even if your yard isn't bathed in sunlight.

TYPES OF SHADE

You'll find different levels of shade and sunlight in different areas of your garden, but there are four basic classifications to consider:

Deep or Full Shade: These are areas with all-day shade and no direct sunlight. This is the most difficult type of shade to work with, especially if the soil is dry because of shallow-rooted trees. You may need to water more frequently to keep plants healthy.

Part Shade: Part-shade gardens are in the shade for part of the day and in

RIGHT: Hostas are a tried and true shade plant that come in many shapes, colors, and sizes.

Comprehensive blueprint packages are available for each of the designs in this chapter. Professionally designed and prepared with precise attention to detail, these easy-to-follow plans include:
- a precise plot plan
- regionalized plant and materials lists
- a plant size and description guide
- installation and maintenance information

These plans will help you or your contractor achieve professional results, adding beauty and value to your property for years. Turn to page 153 for ordering information.

direct sun at other times. These conditions can be tricky to work with, since
many shade plants wilt if they are
in shade in the morning and full sun in
the afternoon; shade plants do better
with morning sun and afternoon shade.
Some sun-loving plants perform well in
part shade.

Light Shade: Light shade consists of
dappled or filtered light created by high-
canopied trees. The soil may be damp or
dry, depending on the type of trees. Many
plants grow well in light shade.

Open Shade: Often occurring in city
gardens or on the north side of suburban
homes, you'll find open shade where no
direct sun falls, although light and heat
may be reflected from surrounding walls.
The soil may be damp or dry.

GARDEN COLOR IN THE SHADE

The light in shaded gardens often has a
cool, bluish or greenish cast that affects
the colors of the plants growing there. Too
many blue and purple flowers in a shade
garden can tend to be gloomy, because

these colors deepen and enhance shadows.
White and pink look wonderful in the
recesses of a shady garden, adding a bright
note that livens up the design. Likewise,
gold, yellow, and chartreuse add touches of
sunny warmth that counteract the cool-
ness of the shadows.

Getting the right amount of color into
a shady site can be difficult, but it's something the designers were keenly aware of
when they created the landscapes in this
chapter. Here are some of their secrets:

There are a number of options to add

LEFT: Hostas are an ideal choice for garden beds that don't receive full sunlight. OPPOSITE: A shady area can be a perfect spot for a dining space or other outdoor getaway.

foliage in tones of pink, white, and green to a shady garden. Plants like "Burgundy Glow" bugleweedbungleweed, coleus, polka-dot plant, caladium, or Japanese painted fern are all good variegated, or multicolored, options. When designing a garden with variegated foliage, be sure to use plenty of quiet greens or blue-greens to provide a calming foil for the busy patterns of multicolored plants. For floral shades of pink and white, consider goat's beard, astilbe, azalea, foamflower, and impatiens.

For sun-kissed tones, try mixing the yellows and golds of flowering and foliage plants. For warm-colored flowers, choose St. John's wort, marsh marigold, daffodil, "Sulphureum" bishop's-hat, English primrose, pansy, yellow flag iris, lemon daylily, "Golden Splendor" lily, and fox-glove. For bright leaves, choose coleus; "Gold Edger," "Gold Standard," and "Golden Tiara" hosta; "Golden Queen" and "Golden King" English holly; and "Goldmound" spirea.

For chartreuse touches, use the vibrant flowers of lady's mantle to echo the edges of "Aureo-marginata" hosta. Or combine the brilliant flowers of cushion spurge with the delicate yellowish green of full-moon maple leaves.

One particularly effective color scheme for a shade garden is white, which includes white- and cream-variegated foliage, such as hostas and pulmonarias, and white- and cream-colored flowers, such as impatiens, astilbe, goat's beard, and snakeroot. Or plant a garden with pink-variegated foliage and pink flowers, using impatiens, astilbe, "Rubrum" lily, polka-dot plant, caladium, and coleus. A more subtle and sophisticated theme is a green garden that emphasizes the various colors and textures of foliage. For this type of garden, combine hostas, ferns, and glossy-leaved broadleaf evergreen shrubs.

TEXTURES IN THE SHADE

In deep shade, you may have to depend on foliage color and texture for interest, since the number of flowering plants that grow well under these conditions is limited. That doesn't stop you from having a compelling garden, however. You can create all sorts of subtle, sophisticated designs using drifts of foliage plants in varying textures, from bold to delicate. You can also enhance textural contrasts by choosing neighboring plants with contrasting foliage color and by repeating a color farther away.

For example, the immense, glossy chartreuse to gold leaves of a "Sum & Substance" hosta can be used to repeat the color of the fine-textured but equally bright leaves of "Limemound" and "Goldmound" spirea. Plant a green hosta, such as lance-leaf Hosta, and a green fern, such as cinnamon fern, between these plants to emphasize the differing colors and textures.

As you can see, selecting plants for a shady site can be a challenging task. The

PLANTS FOR SHADE

Creating a successful shade garden starts with plant selection. Here are some popular choices, all of which can thrive in something between deep and open shade.

ANNUALS & TENDER BULBS
Begonia (*Begonia sempervirens*)
Caladium (*Caladium x hortulanum*)
Clivia (*Clivia miniata*)
Coleus (*Solenostemon scutelloides*)
Edging lobelia (*Lobelia erinus*)
Impatiens (*Impatiens wallerana*)
Sweet alyssum (*Lobularia maritima*)

GROUNDCOVERS
Bishop's-hat (*Epimedium sulphureum*)
English ivy (*Hedera helix*)
Foamflower (*Tiarella cordifolia*)
Lily-of-the-valley (*Convallaria majalis*)
Myrtle/periwinkle (*Vinca minor*)
Sweet woodruff (*Galium odoratum*)

SHRUBS
Azalea (*Rhododendron spp.*)
Japanese andromeda (*Pieris japonica*)
Mountain laurel (*Kalmia latifolia*)
Rhododendron (*Rhododendron spp.*)
Sweet box (*Sarcococca hookerana var. humilis*)
Yew (*Taxus spp.*)

PERENNIALS & HARDY BULBS
Astilbe (*Astilbe x arendsii*)
Bleeding heart (*Dicentra spectabilis*)
Columbine (*Aquilegia canadensis*)
Dead nettle (*Lamium maculatum*)
Fern (*various genera and species*)
Forget-me-not (*Myosotis sylvatica*)
Foxglove (*Digitalis purpurea*)
Goat's beard (*Aruncus dioicus*)
Hosta (*Hosta species and cultivars*)
Japanese anemone (*Anemone x hybrida*)
Lady's mantle (*Alchemilla x hybrida*)
Lenten rose (*Helleborus orientalis*)
Lily (*Lilium spp.*)
Primrose (*Primula spp.*)
Solomon's seal (*Polygonatum odoratum*)
Sweet violet (*Viola odorata*)

landscape designers who created the plans in this chapter have done the hard work for you, however. When you order the blueprints for one of these plans, you'll receive a customized list of plants selected to succeed in a shady site, and in your geographic region. ■

SHADE-LOVING PLANTS

plan# HPT94023

SHOWN IN SPRING
DESIGN BY MICHAEL J. OPISSO

SEE PAGE 153 TO ORDER OUR COMPREHENSIVE BLUEPRINT PACKAGE, INCLUDING A REGIONAL-IZED PLANT AND MATERIALS LIST AND OTHER INVALUABLE INFORMATION TO HELP YOU CREATE THIS LANDSCAPE.

Shaded yards need not be dark and dull, as this backyard design demonstrates. Here, beneath the shadows of seven mature trees, a colorful collection of shade-loving shrubs, perennials, and groundcovers flourishes.

Plan View

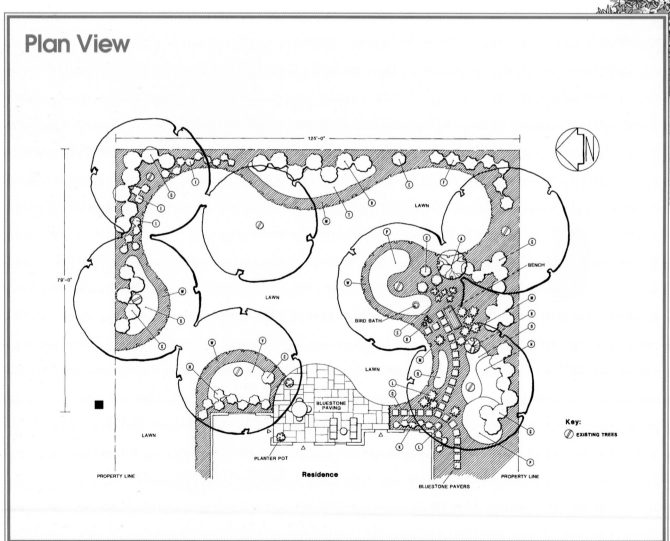

Woe to the gardener who has to deal with established tall trees that cast a great deal of shade—a beautiful, colorful backyard is out of the question, right? Wrong! Nothing could be further from the truth, as demonstrated by this artfully designed shade garden.

The key to working with large existing trees is in using the shade as an asset, not as a liability, and in choosing shade-loving plants to grow beneath them. If the trees have a very dense canopy, branches can be selectively removed to thin the trees and create filtered shade below.

In this plan, the designer shapes the lawn and beds to respond to the locations of the trees. Note that all but one of the trees are situated in planting beds, not in open lawn. Placing a single tree in

the lawn helps to integrate the lawn and planting beds, creating a cohesive design. At the right, the deep planting area is enhanced by pavers, a bench, and a birdbath, creating an inviting, shady retreat. Near the house, a small patio provides a lounging spot; its curving shape echoes the curving form of the planting beds.

Throughout the garden, perennials, woody plants, and groundcovers are arranged in drifts to create a comfortable and serene space. The garden is in constant but ever-changing bloom from early spring through fall, as its special plants—chosen because they thrive in just such a shady setting in their native habitats—go in and out of bloom. Fall brings big splashes of foliage color to complete the year-long show. To provide the finishing carpet to this beautiful and cool shade garden, choose a grass-seed variety selected to tolerate shade.

PERFECT PERGOLA

Sitting in the open shade cast by the pergola evokes the secure feeling of being in an outdoor room where you can fully enjoy the flowers in the surrounding garden. This plan's designer enhances the feeling of an outdoor room by adding lattice panels to the ends of the pergola, enclosing it further and providing the perfect place for a colorful cover of climbing vines.

Meant to be situated in an open area of the yard, this pergola planting creates a decorative centerpiece in the lawn—you can

site it in either the front- or backyard. To prevent the pergola from looking too massive and dominant, the designer adds several tall trees to the bed, off-setting and balancing its size and shape and anchoring it to the surrounding landscape.

The flagstone patio under the pergola has two entrance paths from the lawn—one on each long side—so that you can walk through the garden. That way, the large island planting becomes a lovely destination rather than an obstacle in the middle of the lawn.

Plan View

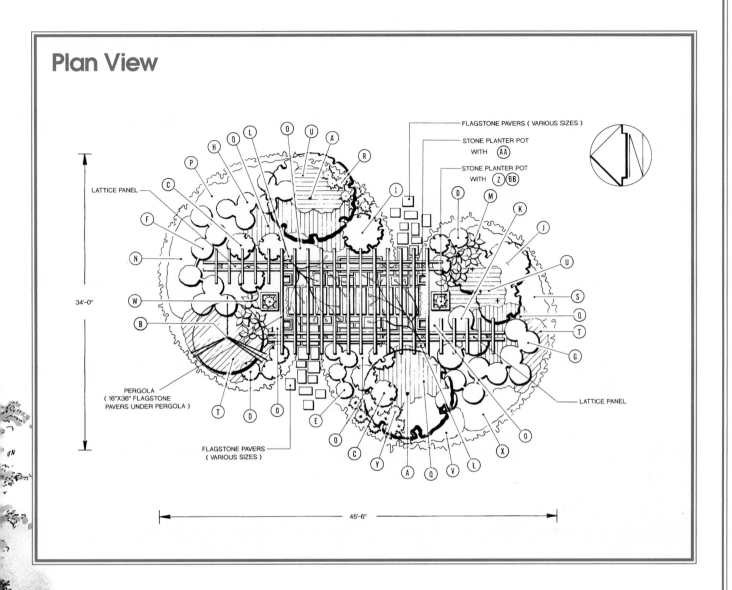

FLAGSTONE PAVERS (VARIOUS SIZES)

STONE PLANTER POT WITH (AA)

STONE PLANTER POT WITH (Z)(BB)

LATTICE PANEL

34'-0"

PERGOLA
(16"X36" FLAGSTONE
PAVERS UNDER PERGOLA)

FLAGSTONE PAVERS
(VARIOUS SIZES)

LATTICE PANEL

45'-6"

Site this beautiful pergola and its surrounding garden bed at a distance from the house, where it creates a dramatic focal point that draws visitors to come and explore.

plan # HPT94024

SHOWN IN SUMMER
DESIGN BY FRANK ESPOSITO

SEE PAGE 153 TO ORDER OUR COMPREHENSIVE BLUEPRINT PACKAGE, INCLUDING A REGIONALIZED PLANT AND MATERIALS LIST AND OTHER INVALUABLE INFORMATION TO HELP YOU CREATE THIS LANDSCAPE.

SERENE RETREAT

plan # HPT94025

SHOWN IN SPRING
DESIGN BY MARIA MORRISON

SEE PAGE 153 TO ORDER OUR COMPREHENSIVE BLUEPRINT PACKAGE, INCLUDING A REGIONALIZED PLANT AND MATERIALS LIST AND OTHER INVALUABLE INFORMATION TO HELP YOU CREATE THIS LANDSCAPE.

A shady front- or backyard can be transformed into a lovely garden setting by planting this undulating border beneath the existing trees. Modify the plan to suit the locations of your existing trees and dig planting holes for shrubs only where you will not sever tree roots that are thicker than one inch in diameter.

Plan View

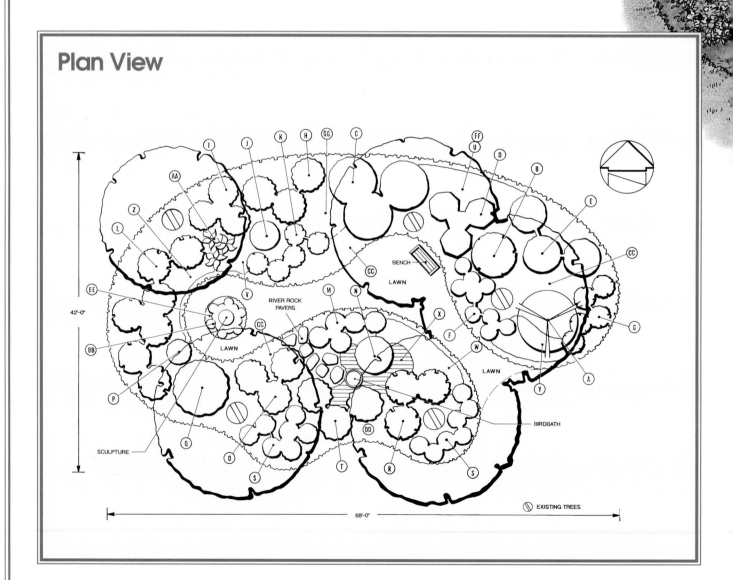

The roughly C-shaped design of this shady bed creates an eye-pleasing curve. The garden's undulating interior edge forms all kinds of interesting nooks and crannies, which invite visitors to explore. Site this bed under the spread of high-canopied trees, which offer filtered shade—the kind that allows many types of shade-loving plants to flourish.

Shade-loving shrubs dominate the bed, with drifts of spring-flowering bulbs, colonies of ferns, and groups of perennials interspersed throughout to add more color. Bulbs dot the mulched areas between

the shrubs in spring. Once the bulbs finish their display and go dormant, the mulch serves as pathways into the rest of the bed.

Many of the shrubs have lovely flowers during spring and summer, followed by showy berries that appear in fall and persist through winter. The designer adds a birdbath to accommodate the birds attracted by the berry-producing shrubs. Structural elements include a garden sculpture and a stepping-stone path that leads to a rustic bench, where visitors can sit and enjoy the naturalistic setting.

COLORFUL CURVES

plan # HPT94026

SHOWN IN SUMMER
DESIGN BY SUSAN A. ROTH

SEE PAGE 153 TO ORDER OUR COMPREHENSIVE BLUEPRINT PACKAGE, INCLUDING A REGIONAL-IZED PLANT AND MATERIALS LIST AND OTHER INVALUABLE INFORMATION TO HELP YOU CREATE THIS LANDSCAPE.

Designed for a location where sunlight is insufficient to support most free-flowering plants, this showy border derives its color from an array of shade-loving shrubs and perennials featuring variegated, golden, or purplish-red leaves.

Plan View

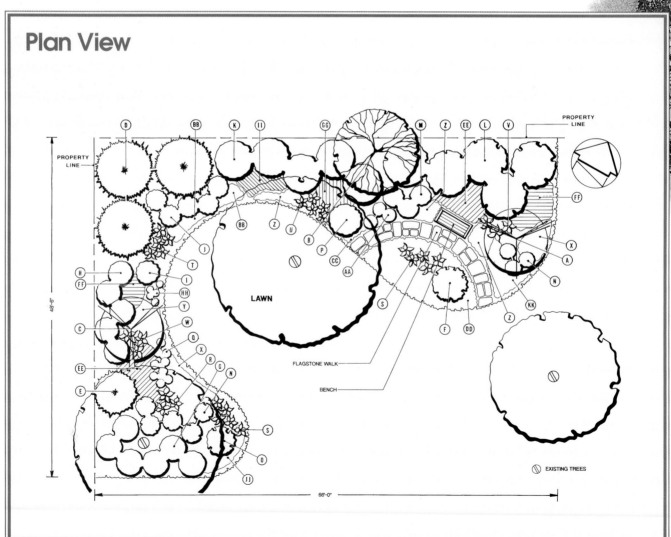

PROPERTY LINE

PROPERTY LINE

LAWN

FLAGSTONE WALK

BENCH

EXISTING TREES

48'-6"

66'-0"

A shade garden need not depend on flowers—which usually need some sun to perform well—for color. You can enliven a shady area with a border that relies on a rainbow of foliage color to provide subtle, yet engaging beauty. An assortment of plants with variegated or unusually tinted foliage, such as burgundy, blue-green, golden yellow, and chartreuse, thrives in shady conditions. This design contains an artful mix of foliage plants with colors and textures that range from understated to bold.

In this gently curving border, the designer combines a variety of deciduous and evergreen shrubs and trees with perennials to provide year-round foliage color. Many of the plants also add floral accents to the design. The simple green of some of the evergreen plants acts as a foil for variegated and colored leaves in the border and helps to create a harmonious scene. A semicircular flagstone path leads to a bench, enticing visitors to sit in the cool shade and enjoy the splendor of the leafy display.

SHADY FLOWER BORDER

plan# HPT94027

SHOWN IN SUMMER
DESIGN BY MICHAEL J. OPISSO

SEE PAGE 153 TO ORDER OUR
COMPREHENSIVE BLUEPRINT
PACKAGE, INCLUDING A REGIONAL-
IZED PLANT AND MATERIALS LIST AND
OTHER INVALUABLE INFORMATION TO
HELP YOU CREATE THIS LANDSCAPE.

This garden of shade-loving plants flourishes under trees where grass struggles to survive. Be sure to keep the plants healthy by providing plenty of water and fertilizer, especially if the garden plants compete for moisture and nutrients with thirsty tree roots.

Plan View

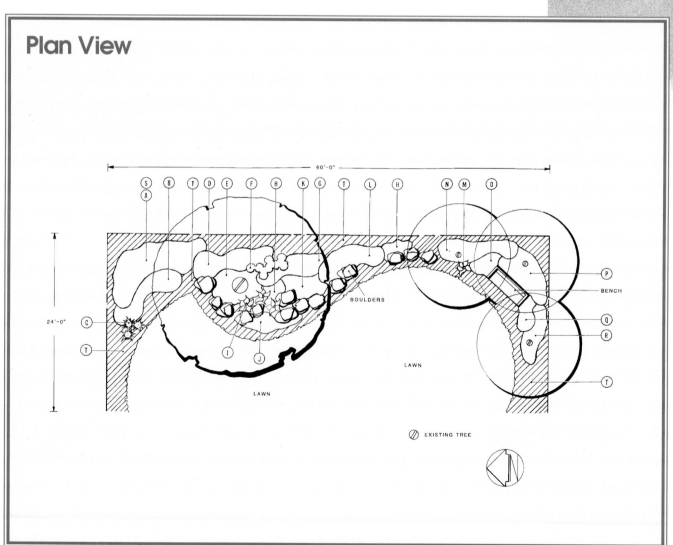

BOULDERS

BENCH

LAWN

LAWN

⦸ EXISTING TREE

If you're constantly complaining that nothing will grow in the shade of the trees in your backyard, consider planting this beautiful shady flower border. Lawn grass needs full sun and struggles to grow under trees, so why not plant something that flourishes in the shade and looks much prettier! This charming flower border features shade-loving perennials and ferns, fits under existing trees, and blooms from spring through fall. In this design, flowering perennials grow through a low evergreen groundcover, which keeps the garden pretty even in winter, when the perennials are dormant.

Also providing year-round interest are rocks and boulders, as well as a bench that invites you to sit and enjoy the pretty scene. The designer shows this garden against a fence along the property border, but you could plant it in front of a hedge or other shrubbery and place it anywhere in your yard. If your property is smaller, you can easily eliminate the corner containing the bench and end the border with a trio of rocks.

CHAPTER 7

Private Oasis
Landscapes Featuring Water

From pools and ponds to waterfalls, streams, and fountains, water can be a powerful focal point in your garden. Water captivates the eye with pools of mirrored images that reflect earth and sky. Soothing sounds—from a gentle breeze rippling through still waters to the compelling rush of a waterfall—become music to one's ears.

Imagine the refreshing appeal of a cooling waterfall on a hot summer's day, the relaxing effects of a gurgling stream, or the quiet reflections of a tranquil pool. Now stop imagining, and start planning for an irresistible sensory experience that only water can add to your yard.

Deciding on a particular water feature begins with simply looking at your surroundings. The landscapes featured in this chapter each include elements that fit naturally with the designs around them, but you'll want to be sure to select one that fits in your specific space. If you want to take full advantage of your kitchen view of a wooded backyard landscape, for example, a naturalistic pond may be ideal.

When planning a pond, first consider environmental factors such as drainage

RIGHT: Boulders bursting through the water at the pond's edge look natural and conceal the pond's vinyl liner.

Comprehensive blueprint packages are available for each of the designs in this chapter. Professionally designed and prepared with precise attention to detail, these easy-to-follow plans include:
- a precise plot plan
- regionalized plant and materials lists
- a plant size and description guide
- installation and maintenance information

These plans will help you or your contractor achieve professional results, adding beauty and value to your property for years. Turn to page 153 for ordering information.

and runoff. A fertilized lawn bordering a pond could cause problems, since fertilizers promote algae growth and would be harmful to fish, if you plan to add them.

To help keep your pond's ecosystem in balance, locate it somewhere that receives at least four to five hours of sun daily. Add aquatic plants—both oxygenating (submerged) and floating—to help keep algae under control by shading sunlight and consuming nutrients. For best results, cover at least half of the surface area of the pond with floating water plants.

DEPTH CHARGE

Depending on the climate, ponds can be anywhere from six inches to three feet deep. To look as natural as possible, create one with varied depths: perhaps two feet at the center, with two perimeter shelves— from 8 inches to 12 inches deep—created to accommodate water plants and boulders along the edge of the pond.

When designing a pond, you can choose a preformed fiberglass insert, or make a freeform shape with a rubber or plastic liner. Using a liner allows you to create a more realistic shape, and one that fits your property. Use stones and rocks to conceal the pond's edge; you may even want to place a

OTHER BODIES OF WATER

Naturalistic ponds are among the most popular water features to add to our gardens, and you'll find beautiful examples of two landscapes with ponds on the following pages (92 and 96). But it's not your only option when you want to add H_2O to your yard. Also consider:

■ **Swimming pool:** The plan on page 94 features a design for a refreshing pool that's cast in a new light. With waterfalls and an irregular shape, the pool takes on the look of a natural pond, discovered in the wilderness.

■ **Secluded fountain:** Page 98 showcases a semicircular fountain, secluded among a dense backyard planting. With a winding path leading the way, the fountain is the centerpiece that calls you towards its private retreat.

■ **Formal fountain:** Find an idea for your backyard's perfect focal point on page 100. The bubbling fountain and stone patio offer an ideal setting for entertaining: it's spacious, with plenty of room to move, but the fountain keeps the space from feeling empty.

Any of these options offers the unique peace and tranquility that comes with a splash of water on your landscape. Pick the one that's right for you—and your yard—and the benefits will trickle down for years to come.

LEFT: Pond edge plantings and natural-looking stones ease this pond and waterfall into their surroundings with realistic style.

large boulder so that it bursts through the water's surface. Use caution when selecting stones, since irregularly shaped boulders can puncture the liner. Avoid limestone, it contains a mineral that promotes algae growth.

A water pump, along with a skimmer box and a biological filter, will help keep the pond's ecosystem in balance. Ideally, a pump should be able to turn the water over at least once every two to three hours. But a water pump may not be entirely necessary—the proper balance of aquatic plants and fish will help control water clarity even in a quiet pool.

The synergistic relationship works because plants and fish not only provide for each other's needs, but also work together to control algae growth that can otherwise turn water murky. As the fish feed on plant roots and consume oxygen released by the plants, the plants are nourished by the nitrogen-rich fish wastes and carbon dioxide. In fact, when the aquatic network is well-balanced, additional feed for fish and plants is minimal and may not even be needed at all.

WHAT YOUR POND WILL SUPPORT

As a rule of thumb, every square foot of water surface will support the following: one bunch of submerged (oxygenating) plants, about two inches of fish, and one snail (pond scavengers like the Japanese black snail).

Floating plants—which provide a safe haven for fish and keep algae under control by shading the water—should cover about 50 percent of the pond surface. You should increase the ratio slightly for smaller water features and those located in sunny areas.

Take note that the ecosystem can become unbalanced when oxygen levels decline, a condition usually caused by an excess of fish or plant material covering the water surface. If changing those numbers doesn't provide a quick solution, you'll need to revive your pond with a circulation and filtration system.

Maintenance issues are usually minimal once the balance of plants, fish, and other aquatic life—microscopic and otherwise—has been established. If your pond includes a filter, you will need to clean it on a monthly or yearly basis, depending on the type of filter and the size of your pond. In the summer, excessive evaporation can occur, causing water levels to drop by as much as an inch per week. Check the water level often and add small amounts as needed. When autumn arrives, skim fallen leaves from the water's surface and remove any debris from around the pump to keep the water clean. ■

COOL POOL

plan# HPT94028

SHOWN IN SUMMER
DESIGN BY DAMON SCOTT

SEE PAGE 153 TO ORDER OUR COMPREHENSIVE BLUEPRINT PACKAGE, INCLUDING A REGIONALIZED PLANT AND MATERIALS LIST AND OTHER INVALUABLE INFORMATION TO HELP YOU CREATE THIS LANDSCAPE.

Resembling a tranquil country pond high in the mountains, this swimming pool, with its waterfalls, river-rock paving, and border planting, brings a wonderful, natural setting to your own backyard.

Plan View

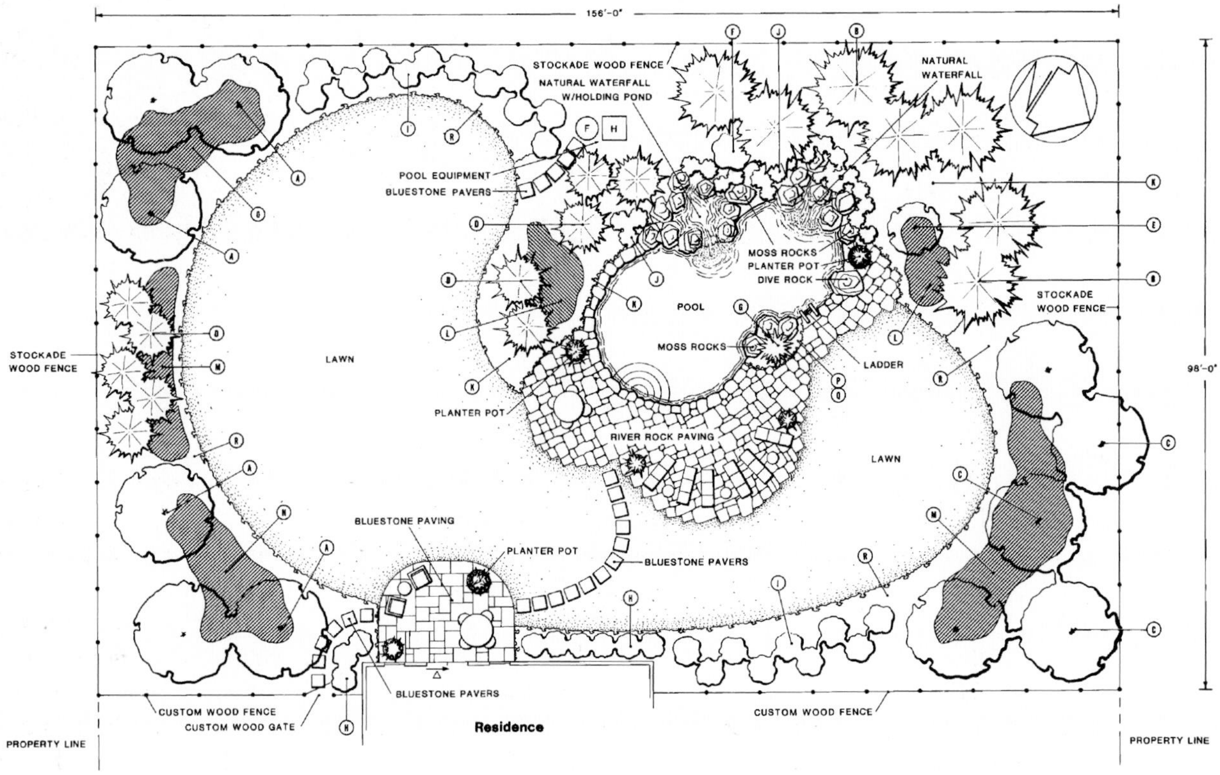

156'-0"

98'-0"

STOCKADE WOOD FENCE
NATURAL WATERFALL W/HOLDING POND

NATURAL WATERFALL

POOL EQUIPMENT
BLUESTONE PAVERS

MOSS ROCKS
PLANTER POT
DIVE ROCK

POOL

MOSS ROCKS

STOCKADE WOOD FENCE

STOCKADE WOOD FENCE

LAWN

LADDER

PLANTER POT

RIVER ROCK PAVING

LAWN

BLUESTONE PAVING

PLANTER POT

BLUESTONE PAVERS

CUSTOM WOOD FENCE

CUSTOM WOOD FENCE
CUSTOM WOOD GATE

BLUESTONE PAVERS

Residence

PROPERTY LINE

PROPERTY LINE

If you look at this landscape design and ask yourself, "Is that really a swimming pool?" then the designer is to be congratulated because he succeeded in his intention. Yes, it is a swimming pool, but the pool looks more like a natural pond and waterfall—one that you might discover in a clearing in the woods during a hike in the wilderness.

The designer achieves this aesthetically pleasing, natural look by employing several techniques. He creates the pool in an irregular free-form shape and paints it "black," actually a very dark marine blue, to suggest the depths of a lake. Large boulders form the waterfalls, one of which falls from a holding pond set among the boulders. River-rock paving—the type of water-worn rocks that line the cool water of a natural spring or a rushing stream—surrounds the front of the pool. The far side of the pool is planted right to the edge, blending the pool into the landscape. If you want to make a splash, you can even dive into this pool—from a diving rock rather than a diving board.

Although the pool is the main attraction here, the rest of the landscape offers a serene setting with abundant floral and foliage interest throughout the year. For security reasons, a wooden stockade fence surrounds the entire backyard, yet the plantings camouflage it well. The irregular kidney shape of the lawn is pleasing to look at and beautifully integrates the naturalistic pool and landscaping into its man-made setting.

THE NEW AMERICAN GARDEN

Many cultures seem to have an identifiable garden style—there are formal Italian fountain gardens, French parterres, English perennial borders, and Japanese contemplation gardens. For many years, we didn't have an American-style garden. Now, a new trend has arisen, which the originators have dubbed the "New American Garden." This style of landscaping is naturalistic and relies on sweeps of ornamental grasses to create the feel of the prairies that once dominated much of the American landscape.

The backyard garden presented here follows that theme. The grasses used vary from low-growing plants hugging the borders to tall plants reaching six feet or more. Some of the grasses are bold and upright; others arching and graceful. When the grasses flower, they produce plumes that dance in the wind and sparkle in the sun. Foliage colors include bright green, blue-green, variegated, and even blood-red. During autumn, foliage and flowers dry in place, forming a stunning scene of naturalistic hues in varying shades of straw, almond, brown, and rust. Most of the grasses remain interesting to look at all winter, unless heavy snow flattens them to the ground. In early spring, the dried foliage must be cut off and removed to make way for the new growth—but this is the only maintenance chore required by an established garden of ornamental grasses!

The design includes a large realistic-looking pond, which can be made from a vinyl-liner or concrete. At the end of the path leading from the bridge, a small seating area provides retreat.

Plan View

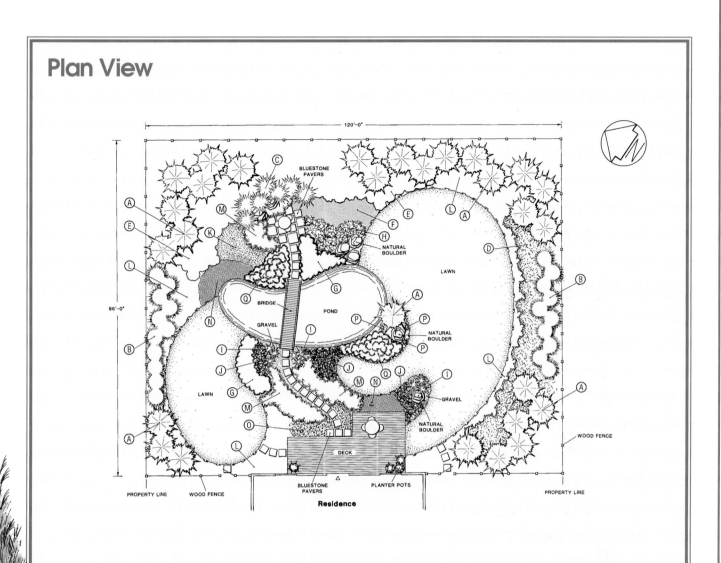

Low in maintenance requirements and high in natural appeal, this garden of ornamental grasses delights the senses all year with subdued foliage colors, sparkling flower plumes, and rustling leaves.

plan# **HPT94029**

SHOWN IN SUMMER
DESIGN BY DAMON SCOTT

SEE PAGE 153 TO ORDER OUR COMPREHENSIVE BLUEPRINT PACKAGE, INCLUDING A REGIONALIZED PLANT AND MATERIALS LIST AND OTHER INVALUABLE INFORMATION TO HELP YOU CREATE THIS LANDSCAPE.

CENTERPIECE POND

plan # HPT94030

SHOWN IN SPRING
DESIGN BY SALVATORE A. MASULLO

SEE PAGE 153 TO ORDER OUR COMPREHENSIVE BLUEPRINT PACKAGE, INCLUDING A REGIONALIZED PLANT AND MATERIALS LIST AND OTHER INVALUABLE INFORMATION TO HELP YOU CREATE THIS LANDSCAPE.

Plant this lovely pond garden where its shade-loving plants will flourish. You'll enjoy the beauty of this design all year long.

Plan View

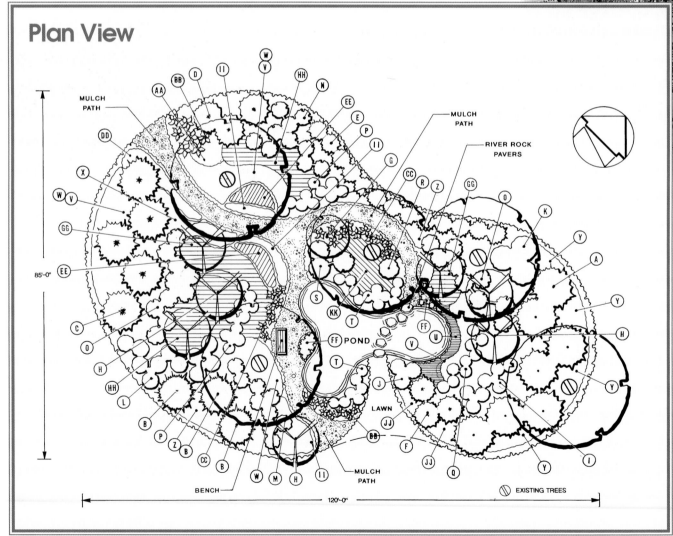

MULCH PATH

MULCH PATH

RIVER ROCK PAVERS

85'-0"

POND

LAWN

BENCH

MULCH PATH

120'-0"

⊘ EXISTING TREES

ORDER BLUEPRINTS 24 HOURS, 7 DAYS A WEEK, AT 1-800-521-6797

Designed to be an oasis in the shade, these garden beds surround a dramatic, yet naturalistic focal point—a small pond. The three lobes of the centrally located pond dictate the rhythm and design concept of the surrounding beds. Visitors enter via one of three entrances that divide the garden into three distinct beds: a large semicircular bed to the northwest, a roughly S-shaped bed to the southwest, and an island bed in the center, nearest the pond. Stepping-stones, set on a slightly sunken ridge, cut across the pond and allow visitors a panoramic view of the garden from the central stone.

Mid-sized evergreens ring the entire garden, giving it a sense of privacy and seclusion. A diverse mix of shade-loving flowering shrubs and trees, ferns, and perennials provide varying texture and color throughout the year.

Site this garden under existing, high-canopied trees. To prevent fallen tree leaves from clogging the pond and fouling the water, cover the pond surface with bird netting in autumn. The black netting is almost invisible and allows you to easily catch and scoop out the leaves.

SECLUDED PATIO

Designed to be a backyard oasis, this mixed garden bed features a gently curving path that leads to a secluded patio and fountain. Deciduous trees and shrubs, evergreens, ornamental grasses, and perennials blend together to create a privacy screen around the seating area. The sense of enclosure is further enhanced with a low berm behind the wall surrounding the fountain. In this intimate setting, you can sit and relax while listening to the music of the splashing fountain.

The designer edged the semicircular fountain basin with stone that matches the patio and walkway to visually unite the design. The varied and dense plantings of this design are attractive to wildlife. As an added bonus, this heavily planted garden leaves little room for pesky weeds to take hold. And because this is a naturalistic garden, there's no need to keep a rigid maintenance schedule. Occasional deadheading and pruning to maintain plant health are the only gardening musts.

Plan View

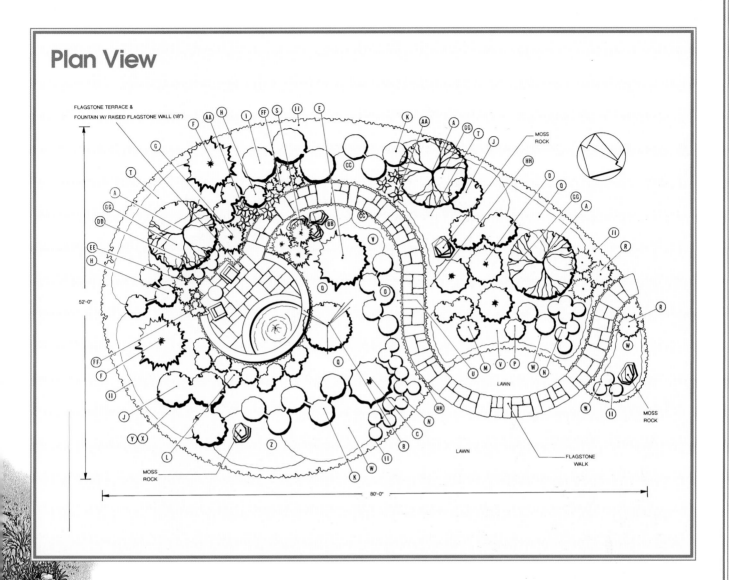

FLAGSTONE TERRACE &
FOUNTAIN W/ RAISED FLAGSTONE WALL (18")

52'-0"

80'-0"

MOSS ROCK

MOSS ROCK

MOSS ROCK

LAWN

LAWN

FLAGSTONE WALK

Sit here in solitude, or with friends and family, and enjoy the sounds of splashing water and singing birds. This bed can be placed almost anywhere on your property to create a beautifully private scene.

plan ⊕ HPT94031

SHOWN IN SUMMER
DESIGN BY JEFFERY DIEFFENBACH

SEE PAGE 153 TO ORDER OUR COMPREHENSIVE BLUEPRINT PACKAGE, INCLUDING A REGIONALIZED PLANT AND MATERIALS LIST AND OTHER INVALUABLE INFORMATION TO HELP YOU CREATE THIS LANDSCAPE.

BUBBLING FOUNTAIN

plan# HPT94032

SHOWN IN SUMMER
DESIGN BY JEFFERY DIEFENBACH

SEE PAGE 153 TO ORDER OUR COMPREHENSIVE BLUEPRINT PACKAGE, INCLUDING A REGIONALIZED PLANT AND MATERIALS LIST AND OTHER INVALUABLE INFORMATION TO HELP YOU CREATE THIS LANDSCAPE.

Relaxing on this patio becomes a delightful sensory experience filled with sweet, flowery fragrances and the music of a bubbling fountain.

Plan View

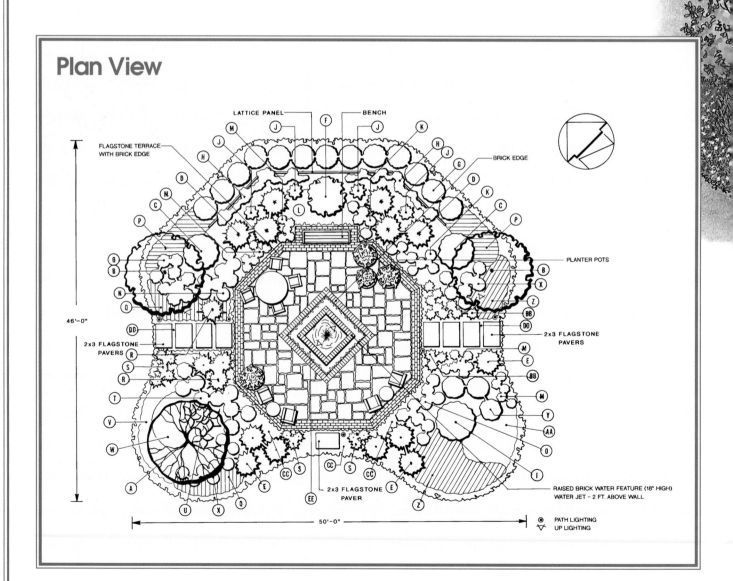

LATTICE PANEL — BENCH

FLAGSTONE TERRACE WITH BRICK EDGE

BRICK EDGE

PLANTER POTS

46'-0"

2x3 FLAGSTONE PAVERS

2x3 FLAGSTONE PAVERS

2x3 FLAGSTONE PAVER

RAISED BRICK WATER FEATURE (18" HIGH) WATER JET - 2 FT. ABOVE WALL

50'-0"

PATH LIGHTING
UP LIGHTING

Imagine being engulfed in delicately scented air as you relax on your patio. You can enjoy such sensory pleasures everyday by installing this intricate design filled with fragrant plants. Be sure to provide plenty of seating around the patio so you'll have places to sit and enjoy the perfumed air.

This plan is as adaptable as it is beautiful. The designer includes a patio and combination fountain/planter, but you could plant the border around any existing patio. You might decide to add only a central planter or fountain, or both. You could locate the design right up against your house so that sliding glass or French doors open directly onto the patio—this allows you to enjoy the flowers' perfume from indoors as well. If you choose this option, site the planting so the lattice is directly opposite the wall of the house to capture and hold fragrance.

The central planter and pots scattered about the patio are filled with fragrant annuals and tender perennials. During the cold winter months, try moving the pots to a sunny location inside the house, where they will continue to bloom and perfume the air.

CHAPTER 8

Garden Party

Yards for Outdoor Entertaining

Large gatherings and warm weather inevitably lead the party outdoors. The right design will not only accommodate a crowd, but will captivate your guests with the colors, scents, and sounds of a fantastic garden.

The primary consideration in designing a backyard for outdoor living is to plan for comfort. The right design will not only accommodate a crowd, but will captivate your guests with the colors, scent, and sounds of a fantastic garden. The designs featured in this chapter were created for people who wish to optimize their use of the outdoors. Each provides plenty of space for family and guests to gather and relax in comfort while enjoying a beautifully planted garden.

You may have an idea of how you would like to use your backyard, but it's worth considering every detail before you select a plan.

■ Will you and your family want to spend hours outdoors sunning and barbecuing, or lounging in the shade?
■ When entertaining, is your style a catered cocktail party or a pot-luck picnic?
■ Do you usually entertain a few close friends, a large gathering of family members, or a group of business acquaintances?
■ Will you be using the yard primarily during the daylight hours, at night, or at all hours?

RIGHT: Family and friends will delight in the enchanting outdoor surroundings of this backyard patio, flanked by flowering vines embracing the pergola.

Comprehensive blueprint packages are available for each of the designs in this chapter. Professionally designed and prepared with attention to detail, these easy-to-follow plans include:
■ a precise plot plan
■ regionalized plant and materials lists
■ a plant size and description guide
■ installation and maintenance information
These plans will help you or your contractor achieve professional results, adding beauty and value to your property for years. Turn to page 153 for ordering information.

THE MAIN OUTDOOR ROOM

Start thinking of your backyard garden as an outdoor living room and plan it accordingly. Think of the area adjacent to the house as a transition space between the indoors and outdoors. Create a large patio or deck there to define the main outdoor living space—the area where you'll be relaxing and entertaining. Easy access from the house to this outdoor living space is crucial, so position it adjacent to doors leading from the kitchen and, if possible, other rooms as well.

Choose a flooring material that complements the architecture of your home and your lifestyle. The choice of wood, stone, or brick for the hardscape will each create a different ambience for the space. Wood seems the most casual and naturalistic, whereas brick and stone look more formal and elegant. You can also mix materials, creating a brick patio a few steps down from a wood deck, as shown in our Love Outdoor Living plan on page 106 or the Carefree Entertaining plan on page 108. In addition to extending the entertaining area, the terraces in these plans provide an easy transition from the deck to the garden.

The most formal design shown in this chapter, our Romantic Outdoor Parties plan on page 114, makes the transition from the house to the backyard with a flagstone patio leading to a formal brick patio. The stunning central fountain is a focal point of the landscape.

If you throw large parties, these designs offer enough room for people to spread across the patio or deck and easily spill out onto the lawn. Unlike the indoor rooms of the house, these outdoor rooms have no walls, so people on the lawn can easily mingle and converse with those on the terrace.

CONTROLLING SUN AND SHADE

Imagine sitting down to lunch at a beautifully set table on a sunny stone terrace in the steamy heat of July. Not very inviting, is it? Although that setting may be perfect for sunbathers, the lunch crowd would bake. All the designs in this chapter include a large deciduous shade tree or two strategically placed near the deck or patio. Because the trees are leafless in spring and late autumn, they allow warming sun to reach the patio during the seasons when the rays feel good, but they cast shade in the summer when you welcome the relief from the sun.

In addition to providing shade, the trees act as a gentle windbreak, keeping the area comfortable in the evening both early and late in the season. The trees featured in these designs won't require constant attention, either—they are situated back into the garden areas so that fallen leaves or flowers don't need to be cleaned up constantly, and designers chose low-maintenance trees that don't constantly shed their leaves.

Anyone who wants to bask in the sun can always move out of the tree's shadow, either onto another part of the terrace or into an open area in the garden. The designs allow for plenty of open, unshaded areas to keep sun worshippers and gardeners happy.

OUTDOOR KITCHENS FOR EASY ENTERTAINING

If you enjoy cooking outdoors and do it frequently, you'll be in your element with a space containing a built-in barbecue, like the one in our Love Outdoor Living plan (page 106). Forget about hauling the grill out of the garage or storage shed—you'll always find it, right where you need it, if you include it in your deck or patio plan.

The added convenience of adjoining service cabinets lets you enjoy outdoor life without constantly running back and forth to the kitchen. You can have placemats, napkins, cutlery, dishes, and barbecue utensils right at your fingertips. When hosting a party, the service cabinets can double as a bar, with extra bottles stored below, and plenty of space for mixing drinks on the countertop.

CREATING A SPECIAL SPOT

A gazebo—like the one in Gracious Gazebo (page 110)—makes an attractive and functional addition to any backyard. Sheltered from the elements, it can be used for an intimate, romantic dinner for two or cocktails for eight or ten. At a larger party, it will lure small groups away from the house and allow them to enjoy the backyard from a different vantage point.

Since a gazebo draws the eye by its shape and size, it acts as a dramatic focal point in the garden. Choose a romantic, gingerbread-style structure for a flowery landscape, or the clean lines of a more contemporary style for a simpler setting. Whichever you choose, you don't want to simply plunk it down in the yard; notice how professional designers tie the gazebo to the landscape with a walk and attractive plantings around it.

ENJOY PRIVACY

While you enjoy your outdoor living room, you may not want to look into your neighbors' homes and yards—or have them watching what you're up to all the time, either. You'll want the freedom to sunbathe or entertain in the privacy of your own backyard without the neighbors ogling your every move.

The landscape designs featured in this chapter use the landscaping to attractively create the privacy you want. Strategically located evergreen trees and shrubs act as stalwart bastions of privacy all year round. They screen views while beautifying the landscape and softening any security fencing behind them.

BRIGHT IDEAS FOR YOUR YARD

You'll need a good lighting plan to enjoy your backyard past sunset, something that's necessary if you plan to entertain in the evening. With the right lighting plan, your outdoor living area can

become even more captivating at night than it is during the day.

Observe the way the light of the sun and the moon play on the landscape and imagine duplicating the effects that you enjoy the most. Pick a focal point of the backyard lighting—a walkway, deck, terrace, large tree, or other part of the landscape. More than two focal points can be confusing, so limit yourself. The rest of the lighting should be softer and built around the focal point.

Using just three basic techniques, you can give a professional look to your backyard at night:

Downlighting, as the name implies, comes from above, simulating the sun or moon depending on the fixtures and the wattage of the bulbs used. This type of lighting works well as safety lighting or basic illumination for pathways, steps, and decks. Be sure to locate fixtures so that

ABOVE: Chairs placed on the lawn in the shade of a tree create an informal, welcoming feeling. **OPPOSITE:** A stepping-stone path invites a stroll toward the patio.

they don't shine directly in your eyes.

In uplighting, the light comes from below, shining dramatically up into the area to be illuminated. Usually floodlights or spotlights are used to uplight a picturesque tree or wall. If the uplighting isn't directly vertical, but angled, it brings out intriguing textures in bark, foliage, walls, and fences.

Backlighting casts indirect silhouettes and shadows created by lighting the surface behind a dark object, such as a tree or a statue. A tree near the house can be backlit by angling the light to shine on the house. The reflected light effectively silhouettes the tree and provides safety lighting. ∎

LOVE OUTDOOR LIVING?

The perfect setting for an outdoor party—or for simply relaxing with family and friends—this backyard features an elegant wooden deck and brick patio that run the length of the house. The deck area on the right (not included in the plans) acts as an outdoor kitchen, featuring a built-in barbecue, serving cabinet, and space enough for a dining table and chairs. For those who opt to mingle with the other guests, rather than chat with the cook, a separate area has been provided at the other end.

Built at the same level as the house, and easily accessible from inside, the deck extends the interior living space to the outdoors. Three lovely flowering trees shade the deck and house, while creating a visual ceiling and walls to further reinforce the idea that these areas are outdoor rooms.

Down a few steps from the deck, the brick terrace makes a transition between the house (and deck) and the garden. Open on two sides to the lawn, this sunny terrace feels spacious and open, creating a great place in which people can mingle and talk during a cocktail party or sunbathe on a Saturday afternoon. From here, it's possible to enjoy the garden setting close at hand. The plantings around the perimeter of the yard feature several kinds of tall evergreens to provide privacy. In front of the evergreens, large drifts of flowering perennials are perfectly displayed against the green background. Between the evergreens, masses of shrubbery provide a changing color show from early spring through fall.

Plan View

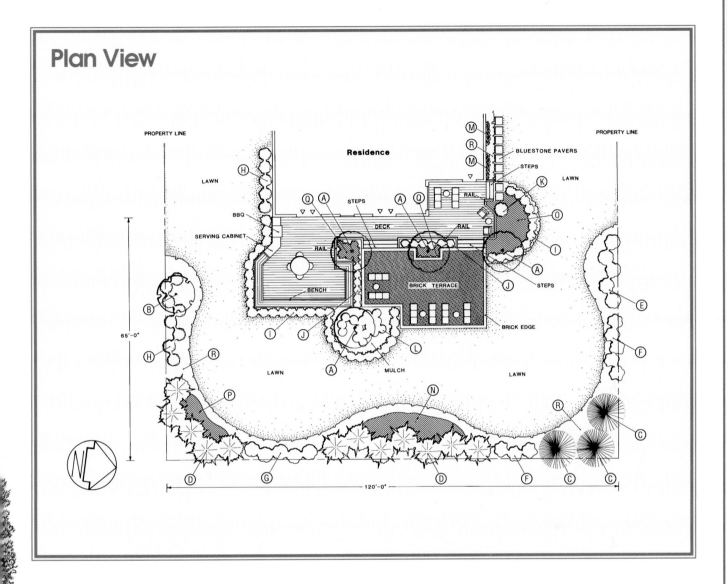

PROPERTY LINE

Residence

LAWN

H

Q A   STEPS   A Q

BBQ

SERVING CABINET

RAIL

DECK

RAIL

RAIL

M

R

M

BLUESTONE PAVERS

STEPS

K

O

I

A

J

STEPS

LAWN

PROPERTY LINE

BENCH

BRICK TERRACE

BRICK EDGE

E

F

B

65'-0"

H

R

I

J

L

A

MULCH

LAWN

N

LAWN

R

C

P

D

G

D

F

C

C

120'-0"

N

Designed for families who love out-door living, this backyard features a deck and patio combination that is perfect for entertaining. It features an area for cooking and dining, as well as space for intimate conversations and relaxing in the sun.

plan# HPT94033

SHOWN IN SPRING
DESIGN BY MICHAEL J. OPISSO

SEE PAGE 153 TO ORDER OUR COMPREHENSIVE BLUEPRINT PACKAGE, INCLUDING A REGIONAL-IZED PLANT AND MATERIALS LIST AND OTHER INVALUABLE INFORMATION TO HELP YOU CREATE THIS LANDSCAPE.

CAREFREE ENTERTAINING

plan# HPT94034

SHOWN IN SUMMER
DESIGN BY MARIA MORRISON

SEE PAGE 153 TO ORDER OUR
COMPREHENSIVE BLUEPRINT
PACKAGE, INCLUDING A REGIONAL-
IZED PLANT AND MATERIALS LIST AND
OTHER INVALUABLE INFORMATION TO
HELP YOU CREATE THIS LANDSCAPE.

Even when there's no action on the
playing court, there's something
exciting going on in this garden.
Designed for year-round interest, the
mixed plantings bordering the lawn
were chosen for colorful flowers, foliage,
or fruit, as well as easy upkeep.

Plan View

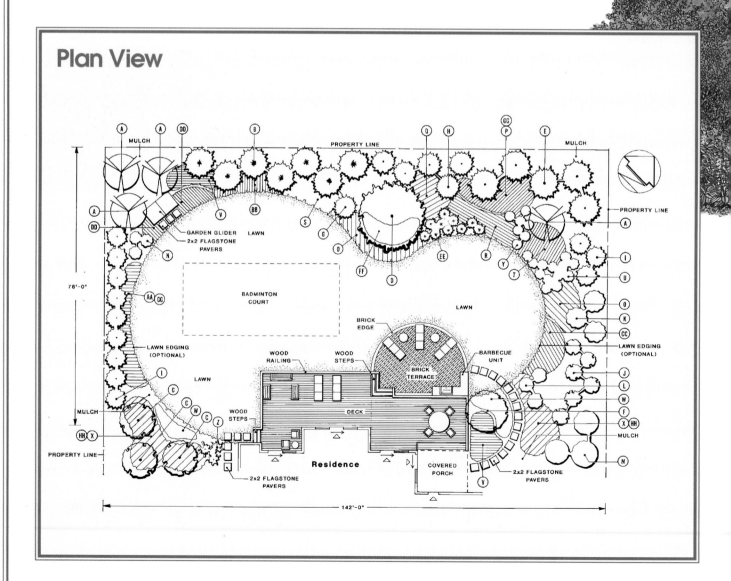

This expansive backyard is designed for entertaining family and friends in a private, relaxing setting. Although the yard measures roughly a quarter of an acre, the overall effect is snug and welcoming. The spacious deck, which runs nearly the width of the house, and the adjoining semicircular brick terrace, allow plenty of room for lounging, dining and visiting with friends. And there's plenty of room for holding large outdoor parties—guests can mingle on the deck and patio and even spill over onto the lawn. Providing maximum convenience, the barbecue unit, a service cabinet, and several benches are built in so they're always accessible.

Shaped for efficient mowing, the gracefully curving lawn is large enough to accommodate a badminton court, croquet game, or all the neighborhood children. And fans will find the roofed garden swing nestled among the plantings, a comfortable grandstand for cheering on their favorite team.

A dramatic purple-leaf weeping tree creates a focal point for the view from the deck and patio. The surrounding plantings include a colorful mix of trees, shrubs, perennials, and bulbs—all chosen for their tidiness or subdued growth. Mulch, which blankets the garden floor to keep down weeds and promote healthy plant growth, is another work-saving measure. Also shown here is deck plan ODA019 by Home Planners. For more information about ordering blueprints for this deck, call 1-800-521-6797.

GRACIOUS GAZEBO

The yard and garden pictured here would delight any flower lover, since they are designed to bloom from early spring into fall. During spring, flowering trees and shrubs, which border part of the property, provide seasonal color.

The main feature of the property, however, is a dramatic perennial border designed to bloom from summer through fall. The key to creating a successful display of flowering perennials lies in choosing and combining plants that bloom together and in sequence, so the garden is never bare of flowers. When so orchestrated, the border displays a fascinating, ever-changing collection of colors. The perennials grow in large drifts to create the most impact when viewed from across the lawn. The planting beds surround an irregular, bow-shaped lawn, a pretty way to add interest to an uninspiring squared-off property.

A low stone wall raises the planting beds several steps up, bringing the flowers closer to eye level and emphasizing the contours of the design. The low retaining wall also provides an attractive way to deal with a sloping property so the lawn can be level. If your property is flat, the wall can be eliminated without altering the basic design. Behind the perennial garden, evergreens form a background that sets off the colors in summer. When sitting on the patio of this beautiful yard, the eye is drawn toward the gazebo. Accessible by a stepping-stone walk, the gazebo makes a wonderful place to sit and relax in the shade while enjoying the beauty of the perennials from a different perspective.

Plan View

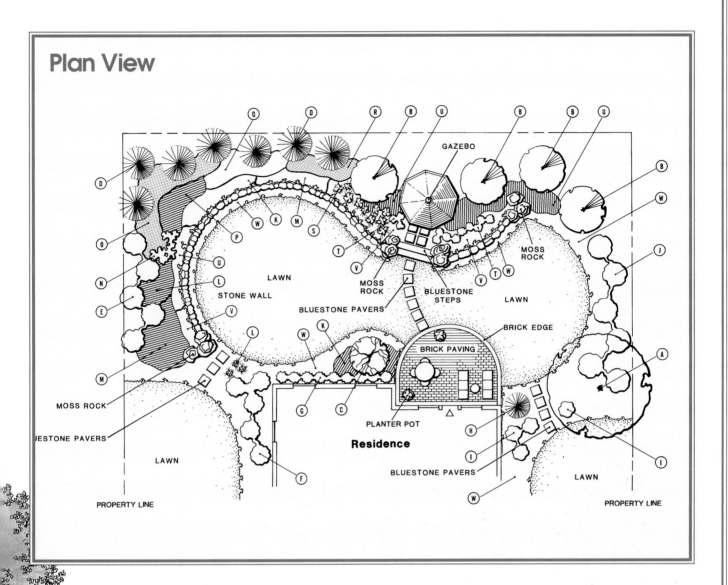

GAZEBO

MOSS ROCK

MOSS ROCK

LAWN

STONE WALL

BLUESTONE PAVERS

BLUESTONE STEPS

LAWN

BRICK EDGE

BRICK PAVING

MOSS ROCK

BLUESTONE PAVERS

LAWN

PLANTER POT

Residence

BLUESTONE PAVERS

LAWN

LAWN

PROPERTY LINE

PROPERTY LINE

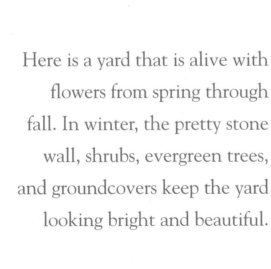

Here is a yard that is alive with flowers from spring through fall. In winter, the pretty stone wall, shrubs, evergreen trees, and groundcovers keep the yard looking bright and beautiful.

plan # HPT94035

SHOWN IN SUMMER
DESIGN BY MICHAEL J. OPISSO

SEE PAGE 153 TO ORDER OUR COMPREHENSIVE BLUEPRINT PACKAGE, INCLUDING A REGIONALIZED PLANT AND MATERIALS LIST AND OTHER INVALUABLE INFORMATION TO HELP YOU CREATE THIS LANDSCAPE.

STUNNING LAWN

plan # HPT94036

SHOWN IN LATE SUMMER
DESIGN BY DAMON SCOTT

SEE PAGE 153 TO ORDER OUR COMPREHENSIVE BLUEPRINT PACKAGE, INCLUDING A REGIONALIZED PLANT AND MATERIALS LIST AND OTHER INVALUABLE INFORMATION TO HELP YOU CREATE THIS LANDSCAPE.

A low deck makes an excellent vantage point for surveying this naturalistic garden, which showcases a beautiful selection of flowers and ornamental grasses.

Plan View

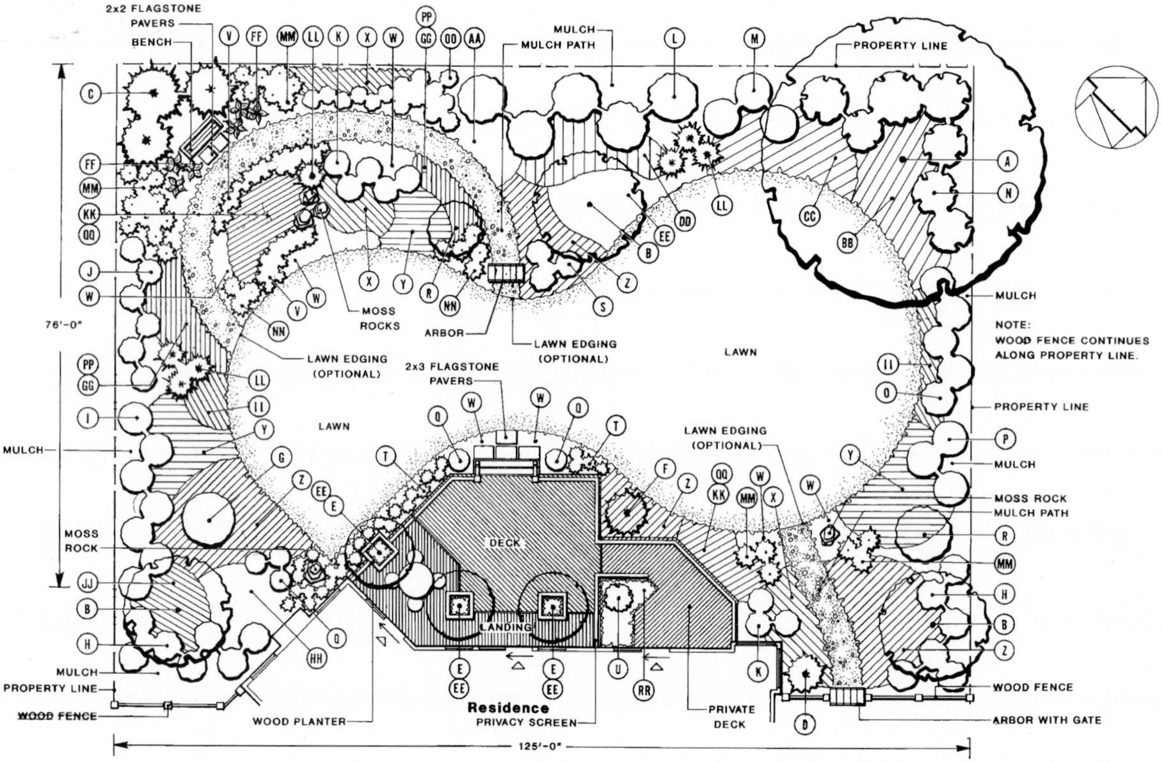

2x2 FLAGSTONE PAVERS
BENCH
MULCH MULCH PATH
PROPERTY LINE
76'-0"
MULCH
MOSS ROCKS
LAWN EDGING (OPTIONAL)
2x3 FLAGSTONE PAVERS
ARBOR
LAWN EDGING (OPTIONAL)
LAWN
LAWN
LAWN EDGING (OPTIONAL)
MOSS ROCK
MULCH
PROPERTY LINE
WOOD FENCE
WOOD PLANTER
DECK
LANDING
Residence
PRIVACY SCREEN
PRIVATE DECK
125'-0"
MULCH
NOTE: WOOD FENCE CONTINUES ALONG PROPERTY LINE.
PROPERTY LINE
MULCH
MOSS ROCK MULCH PATH
WOOD FENCE
ARBOR WITH GATE

To integrate the deck more fully with the landscape and to provide light shade, the designer places several low-maintenance trees in planting pockets in the deck. A graceful arbor positioned straight across from the deck stairs beckons strollers to meander along the semicircular path, where they'll encounter a bench inviting them to sit for a spell. The bench supplies respite and a different perspective from which to admire the garden.

An assortment of plants rings the "figure-eight" lawn, which forms the hub of the landscape. Instead of more traditional groundcovers, drifts of blooming perennials and ornamental grasses blanket the ground. The various plants, chosen for a succession of bloom and carefully interspersed to camouflage the dying foliage of dormant spring bulbs, provide a kaleidoscope of color from season to season.

Besides lawn mowing, the only maintenance you'll need to perform is to cut back and remove the dead foliage once a year in late winter. To reduce upkeep further, a low-care groundcover could be substituted for the turf, and a slightly curving, mulched path installed from the deck stairs to the arbor to accommodate foot traffic. The spacious deck offers a comfortable vantage point for enjoying the flowers and foliage. Mulched planting beds keep this garden free of most weeds, and if the optional lawn edging is installed, the only regular maintenance chore will be lawn mowing.

ROMANTIC OUTDOOR PARTIES

Want to play a role from The Great Gatsby? Then close your eyes and imagine being a guest at a large party in this magnificent garden designed for formal entertaining. Imagine standing in the house at the French doors, just at the entrance to the paved area, and looking out at this perfectly symmetrical scene. The left mirrors the right; a major sight line runs straight down the center past the fountain to the statue that serves as a focal point at the rear of the garden. Three perfectly oval flowering trees on each side of the patio frame the sight line, as well as help to delineate the pavement from the planted areas of the garden.

The flagstone patio along the house rises several steps above the brick patio, giving it prominence and presenting a good view of the rest of the property. The change in paving materials provides a separate identity to each area, yet by edging the brick with bluestone to match the upper patio, the two are tied together.

Pink and purple flowering shrubs and perennials provide an elegant color scheme throughout the growing season. A vine-covered lattice panel, featuring royal purple flowers that bloom all summer long, creates a secluded area accessible by paving stones at the rear of the property. What a perfect spot for a romantic rendezvous!

Plan View

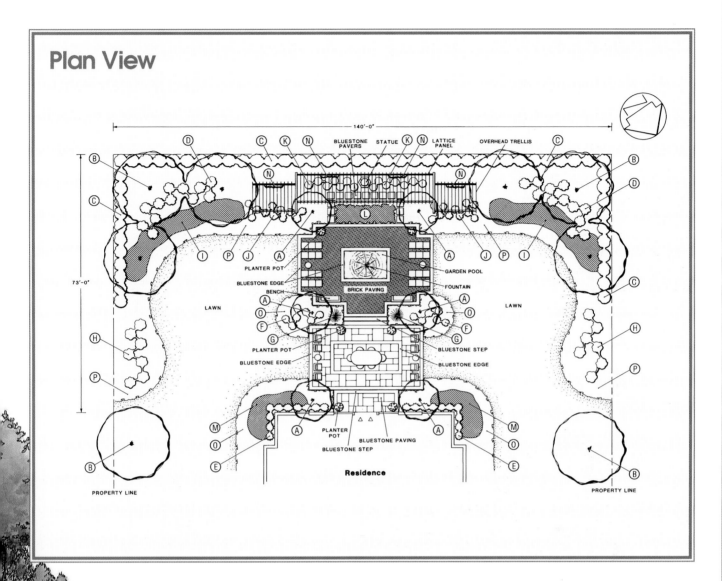

140'-0"

73'-0"

D C K N BLUESTONE PAVERS STATUE K N LATTICE PANEL OVERHEAD TRELLIS C

B N N B

C D

L C

PLANTER POT I P J A A J P I GARDEN POOL

BLUESTONE EDGE BRICK PAVING FOUNTAIN

BENCH A A

A O O A

F F LAWN

LAWN G G

PLANTER POT BLUESTONE STEP

BLUESTONE EDGE BLUESTONE EDGE

H H

P P

M M

A A

O O

PLANTER POT BLUESTONE PAVING

B B

BLUESTONE STEP

E E

Residence

PROPERTY LINE PROPERTY LINE

This formal garden provides
a perfect setting for romantic
outdoor parties or for simply
relaxing in the sun on a
Saturday afternoon.

plan # HPT94037

SHOWN IN SUMMER
DESIGN BY MICHAEL J. OPISSO

SEE PAGE 153 TO ORDER OUR
COMPREHENSIVE BLUEPRINT
PACKAGE, INCLUDING A REGIONAL-
IZED PLANT AND MATERIALS LIST AND
OTHER INVALUABLE INFORMATION TO
HELP YOU CREATE THIS LANDSCAPE.

CHAPTER 9

Backyard Getaways
Landscapes with Quiet Retreats

It doesn't take a sprawling country estate to create a peaceful hideaway in your backyard. With the right design, you can enjoy a retreat that offers privacy thanks to its natural surroundings—a place where you can leave your cares behind, put your feet up, and appreciate the scenery.

A well-designed landscape can serve as the entertainment center of your home, a place to host elaborate parties or to provide children with a perfect spot to play. But amid all that excitement, you might need a quiet place that you can call your own—somewhere to escape and get away from it all. If that sounds appealing, you'll love the designs presented in this chapter.

Creating the ideal quiet retreat requires careful planning; if you spend the time to think about it now, you'll end up with the perfect spot for rest and relaxation. Consider:

■ Where on your property do you want to situate the retreat?

■ How will you lead people there?
■ How do you plan to use it?
■ What will the sitting area be like?
■ How will you make it secluded?

LOCATION, LOCATION, LOCATION

You'll want to evaluate several factors before you decide where to situate a quiet retreat in your yard. As with real estate, this can be the most important consideration in planning a successful retreat in your landscape. Take a look at not only

RIGHT: An Adirondack-style chair and bench lure visitors to this getaway in the shade of surrounding trees.

Comprehensive blueprint packages are available for each of the designs in this chapter. Professionally designed and prepared with attention to detail, these easy-to-follow plans include:
■ a precise plot plan
■ regionalized plant and materials lists
■ a plant size and description guide
■ installation and maintenance information
These plans will help you or your contractor achieve professional results, adding beauty and value to your property for years. Turn to page 153 for ordering information.

the existing characteristics of your yard, but the space around you as well. If you don't have a fence or natural barrier between you and the next-door neighbor, then the property line won't be the best place to get away from it all.

By definition, it seems most natural to place a quiet retreat in the corner of a yard, and that can certainly be a good spot. But don't restrict yourself to the fringes of the property. With the right design, you can have a relaxing getaway right in the middle of your backyard. Our Perennial Tranquility plan (page 122) shows how beds, trees, and paths can work together to give you privacy in any spot of your yard.

LEAD THE WAY

One important consideration is how you will get to your quiet retreat. An inviting path can light up a landscape, turn everyday walks into unfolding journeys, and transform ordinary gardens into something more exciting.

While paths are certainly practical—they reduce soil compaction, give a sense of direction, and keep feet clean and dry—they also add an aesthetic and emotional appeal to the landscape by creating a mood and inviting people to explore. A winding path can help create the sense of privacy at the end, and lets visitors pause and appreciate the garden around them along the way.

Path materials can range from pine needles, bark, grass, and gravel, to natural stone, brick, wood planks, or concrete paving blocks. The type of surface you choose will set the style for your path, as well as the destination. Naturally, it should complement the existing house and landscape design—bark chips make a good choice for a woodland garden in the country, but not as the main path leading from a traditional Victorian home to an outdoor table setting.

USE IT WISELY

One great thing about creating a peaceful hideaway in your backyard is its multitude of potential uses. Take time to think about how you'd like to use your yard before you choose a design, because how you plan to use it will help dictate the design.

Do you want a place where you can escape with the Sunday paper and a cup of coffee? Or a secondary spot for guests to congregate during parties on the back deck? Perhaps a spot for quiet, candlelit dinners for two, surrounded by a garden in full bloom? You can have all of this—and more—with the right plan.

If you're looking for solitude, you'll want to create a smaller space than if you plan to serve meals there. It's always a good idea to picture yourself using the area before you finalize your plans.

TAKE A LOAD OFF

The right sitting area will help to define your space. A hammock may be your idea of the ultimate in relaxation—check out Weekend Retreat (page 124) if that's the case.

Other seating options include the ever-popular Adirondack chairs, as shown in our Flagstone Terrace plan (page 120), or simple table and chair settings, such as you'll find in Perennial Tranquility (page 122).

Perhaps the most popular option for seating areas are benches, which can fit in seamlessly with their surroundings and offer a spot for one or more people to sit and relax. Our Water Garden (page 126) and Privacy Border (page 128) plans both feature wooden benches; the Privacy Border plan includes a particularly unique design, with a circular bench surrounding a tree.

ABOVE: There is nothing as inviting as a hammock for the ultimate in relaxation. OPPOSITE: A simple sitting area will help to define your space, and provide an area for quiet conversation.

CREATING PRIVACY

Choosing the right location is one way to give your retreat a sense of privacy, but it also needs the right design around it—a combination of natural and man-made surroundings that give it a special, secluded feel.

You'll notice that each of the designs in this chapter utilize trees, especially deciduous ones, to create this sense of slight separation from the rest of the lawn. When fully leafed out, these trees act as a shield from neighbors, wind, and excessive sun.

An arbor can also add a sense of seclusion, especially with plants growing up and over it. The Flagstone Terrace and Weekend Retreat plans utilize arbors nicely for this effect.

You'll also want to be sure not to completely enclose the area. If you have a gazebo tucked in the corner of a garden, for example, you'll want it to be visible from the back of your house. It will create a strong focal point in your landscape and lure people out to explore the garden. ∎

FLAGSTONE TERRACE

Your cares melt away when you enter this very private and tranquil garden through the vine-covered arbor. The designer sites an informal flagstone terrace with two seating areas in a sea of evergreen groundcover, entirely eliminating a lawn and making the garden about as carefree as it can be. Evergreens on the property border create privacy, while airy trees—selected because they cast light shade and are easy to clean up after—create a lacy overhead canopy. The overall effect is serene.

A half-circle rock wall, built of small moss-covered boulders, sets off the larger of the two seating areas and gives dimension to the area. (Five moss rocks on the opposite side of the patio echo and balance the wall.) Several types of perennials spill over the top and sprout from the crevices of the wall, decorating the area with their dainty flowers and foliage and creating a soft, natural look. Large drifts of spring bulbs and other perennials make lovely splashes of color where they grow through the groundcover. Flowering shrubs—many of which also display evergreen leaves—give the garden year-round structure and interest while offering easy-care floral beauty.

The lack of a lawn makes this garden especially easy to care for. The groundcover absorbs most of the leaves that drop from the deciduous trees in autumn, and the terrace can be quickly swept or blown free of leaves and debris, as needed. All you'll need to do is cut off the dead tops of the perennials once a year in late winter.

Plan View

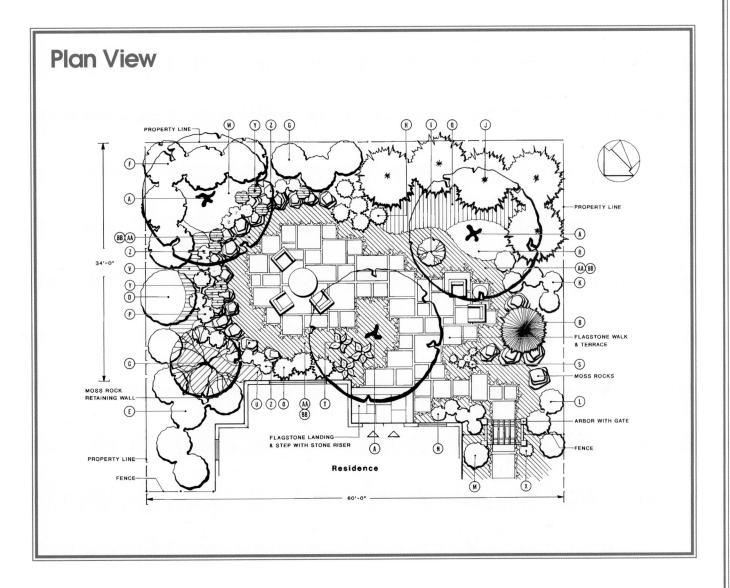

PROPERTY LINE

PROPERTY LINE

34'-0"

MOSS ROCK
RETAINING WALL

PROPERTY LINE

FENCE

FLAGSTONE LANDING
& STEP WITH STONE RISER

FLAGSTONE WALK
& TERRACE

MOSS ROCKS

ARBOR WITH GATE

FENCE

Residence

60'-0"

You'll spend many more hours just relaxing in this backyard retreat than you will taking care of it. Since there's no lawn, you'll escape weekly lawn mowing, and will even be able to leave the garden untended during extended vacations.

plan⊕ **HPT94038**

SHOWN IN SUMMER
DESIGN BY MICHAEL J. OPISSO

SEE PAGE 153 TO ORDER OUR COMPREHENSIVE BLUEPRINT PACKAGE, INCLUDING A REGIONAL-IZED PLANT AND MATERIALS LIST AND OTHER INVALUABLE INFORMATION TO HELP YOU CREATE THIS LANDSCAPE.

PERENNIAL TRANQUILITY

Designed with the flower-lover in mind, this oasis of flowers and grasses looks great all year. Bright flower colors during spring and summer are followed in fall by the pale, elegant flowers and seed heads of the ornamental grasses. The seed heads and foliage persist until the following spring, decorating the winter landscape with their delicate flower-like plumes and wheat-like fronds. Don't cut the dried grasses back to the ground until just before the new growing season begins, so you can enjoy them all winter.

The garden is formed from three connecting beds, with three paths leading into a central paved area between them. Flagstone pavers, which are interplanted with scented groundcover plants, lead into this central patio. A medium-sized deciduous tree in each bed shapes the flagstones and puts on a brilliant show before dropping leaves in fall. This allows you to add a table and chairs, so you can sit quietly and enjoy the trio of colorful garden beds. Be sure to site this lovely design so that the path is visible from a distance. That way, visitors will be tempted to come and enjoy the patio and surrounding plantings.

ORDER BLUEPRINTS 24 HOURS, 7 DAYS A WEEK, AT 1-800-521-6797

Plan View

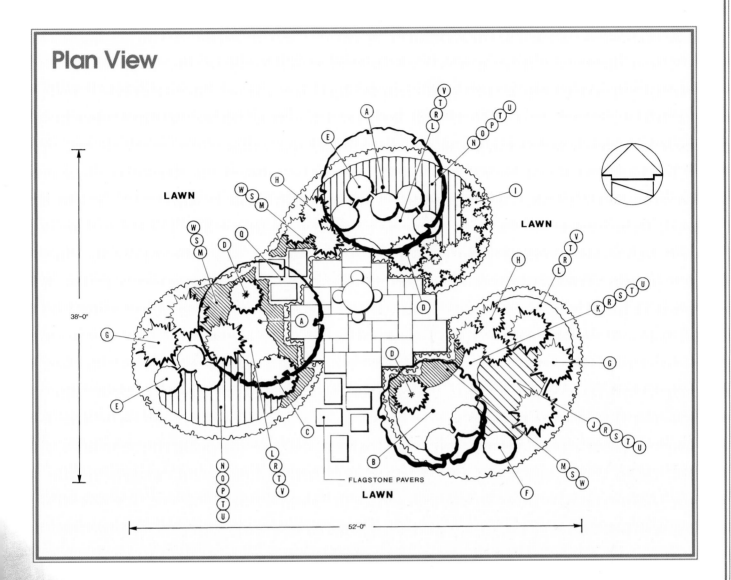

LAWN

LAWN

LAWN

38'-0"

52'-0"

FLAGSTONE PAVERS

You won't be worrying about your gardening chores while sitting on this pretty patio— the flowers and ornamental grasses used here thrive even in poor soil and low moisture.

plan # HPT94039

SHOWN IN SUMMER
DESIGN BY DAMON SCOTT

SEE PAGE 153 TO ORDER OUR COMPREHENSIVE BLUEPRINT PACKAGE, INCLUDING A REGIONALIZED PLANT AND MATERIALS LIST AND OTHER INVALUABLE INFORMATION TO HELP YOU CREATE THIS LANDSCAPE.

WEEKEND RETREAT

plan # HPT94040

SHOWN IN SUMMER
DESIGN BY MICHAEL J. OPISSO

SEE PAGE 153 TO ORDER OUR COMPREHENSIVE BLUEPRINT PACKAGE, INCLUDING A REGIONAL-IZED PLANT AND MATERIALS LIST AND OTHER INVALUABLE INFORMATION TO HELP YOU CREATE THIS LANDSCAPE.

The designer includes large patches of other easy-care perennials that punctuate the rest of the landscape with splashes of color from spring through fall to create a welcoming backyard retreat.

Plan View

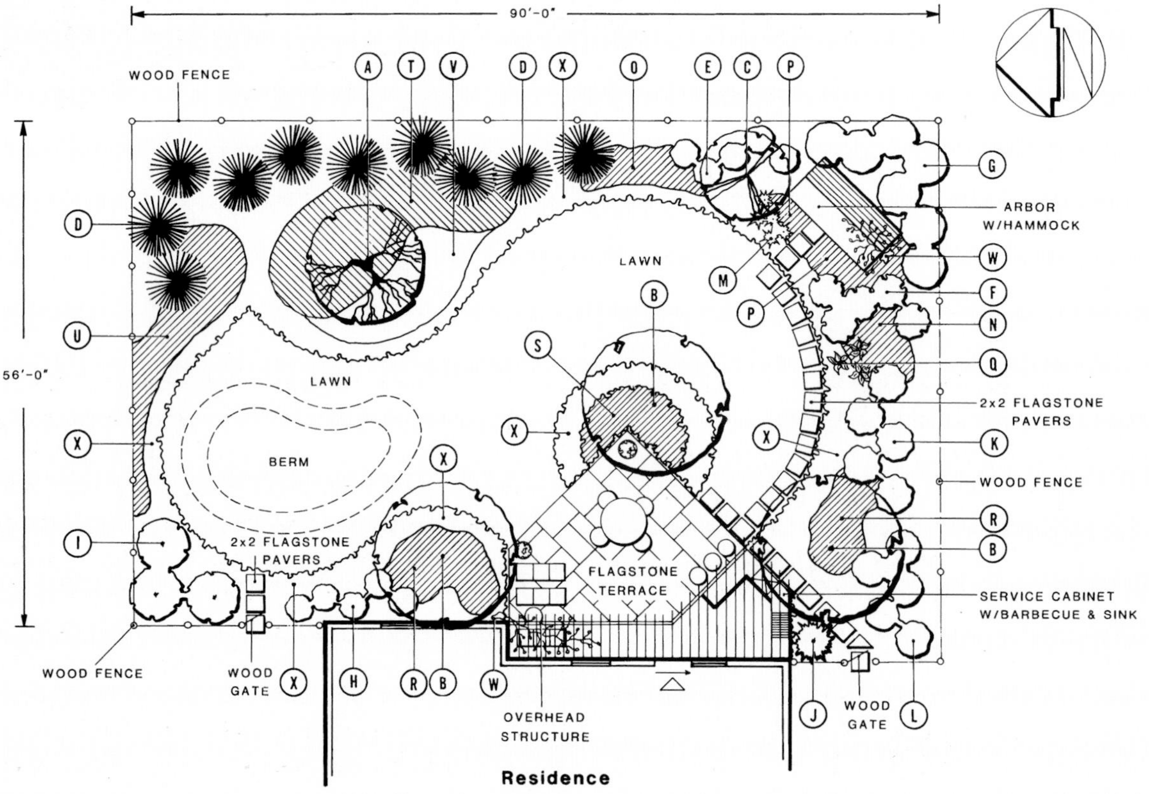

Plan view diagram labeled with:
- 90'-0" (width)
- 56'-0" (height)
- WOOD FENCE
- LAWN
- BERM
- 2x2 FLAGSTONE PAVERS
- WOOD GATE
- OVERHEAD STRUCTURE
- FLAGSTONE TERRACE
- Residence
- ARBOR W/HAMMOCK
- 2x2 FLAGSTONE PAVERS
- WOOD FENCE
- SERVICE CABINET W/BARBECUE & SINK
- WOOD GATE

An arbor-covered hammock and a spacious patio with a kitchen provide comfortable spots for relaxing outdoors while enjoying the colorful flowering perennials. The bermed soil on the left side of the lawn adds dimension and visually counterweights the patio, while providing a complementary curve. This colorful backyard serves as a special weekend retreat where you and your family can spend your free time relaxing and entertaining. Enjoy a quiet afternoon reading or lounging in the hammock under the romantic arbor, or host a cookout for your friends on the spacious patio complete with an outdoor kitchen. Both the patio and the hammock provide refuge from the hot summer sun-a vine-covered overhead trellis and leafy trees protect the patio, and the hammock hideaway tucked in the corner

of the yard can catch a breeze while reflecting the sun's hot rays. Just right for a lazy afternoon snooze, the hammock structure nestles within an intimate flowery setting that encloses and enhances the space. Flagstone pavers lead the way from the patio to the hammock, following the gentle curve of the border, and flagstones mark the entrance from the gates at each side of the yard for easy access. Privacy-protecting evergreen trees and shrubs fill the rear of the property, and all are gracefully set off by a purple-foliaged weeping specimen tree located on sight lines from both the patio and the arbor. (In some regions, another type of eye-catching specimen tree is substituted for the purple-foliaged tree.) For color contrast, long-blooming, yellow flowering perennials surround the tree.

WATER GARDEN

There are few places more tranquil, more relaxing, or more cooling on a hot summer day than a garden with a view of the water—even if the water is no more than a garden pool. In the garden pictured here, two ponds filled with water lilies are used to create a tranquil setting. The first pond is situated near the house, where it is visible from the indoors. The deck is cantilevered over the pond to enhance the closeness of the water, and is covered with an overhead trellis, which ties the two areas together. The trellising also frames the view of the pond from the deck, and of the deck from the garden areas.

A second, smaller pond is set into the corner of the garden and has a backdrop of early-spring flowering trees, ferns, and shade-loving perennials. This intimate retreat is made complete by setting a bench and planter pots beside the pond.

Throughout the property, river-rock paving enhances the natural feeling of the water and provides a sitting area nearby for quiet contemplation. Moss rocks, placed in strategic places in the garden, further carry out the naturalistic theme, as do most of the landscape plants. The shrubs and perennials bordering the undulating lawn provide the needed soft-textured, informal look that makes both ponds seem natural and right at home.

Plan View

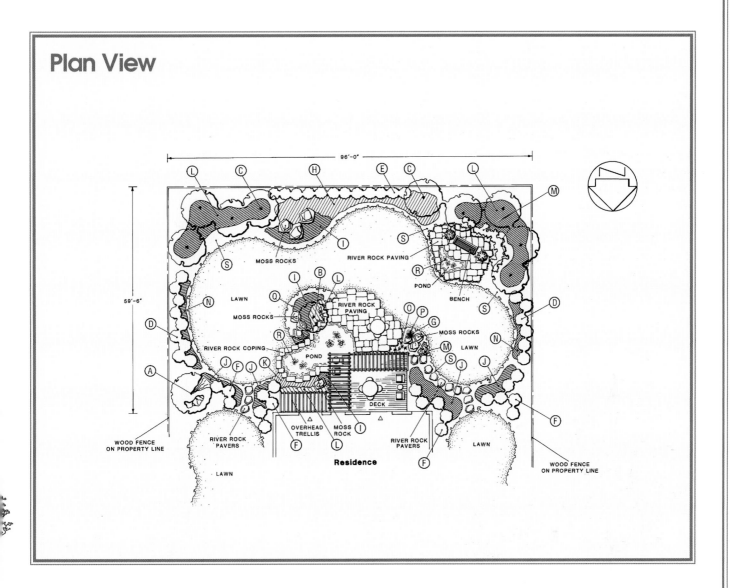

This backyard features not one, but two ponds in which to dip your toes during summer's heat. If you choose to keep your shoes on, sit on the patio near the large pond or on the bench by the small one to cool off in the reflection of the colorful surroundings.

plan# **HPT94041**

SHOWN IN SUMMER
DESIGN BY SUSAN A. ROTH

SEE PAGE 153 TO ORDER OUR COMPREHENSIVE BLUEPRINT PACKAGE, INCLUDING A REGIONALIZED PLANT AND MATERIALS LIST AND OTHER INVALUABLE INFORMATION TO HELP YOU CREATE THIS LANDSCAPE.

PRIVACY BORDER

If you'd like to create a private haven in your backyard without putting up a fence, this plan is for you. This backyard border relies solely on massed plantings of evergreen and deciduous trees and shrubs to screen out neighboring properties and to buffer noise. The designer also includes a charming circular bench where you can sit and enjoy a peaceful yard under the shade of a tree. Edged with flowering groundcovers and bulbs, the circular bed and the main border fit together naturally like puzzle pieces.

Starting with spring-flowering bulbs, this border design offers varied color and texture throughout the year. Broad-leaved and needle-leaved evergreens at the back of the border provide a permanent structure, effective screening and a pleasantly neutral color that sets off the vibrant perennials and bulbs planted in the front. The stepping stones leading through the flowering groundcovers at the tree's base encourage visitors to meander across the lawn to get a closer look at the abundant plantings in the main border.

Plan View

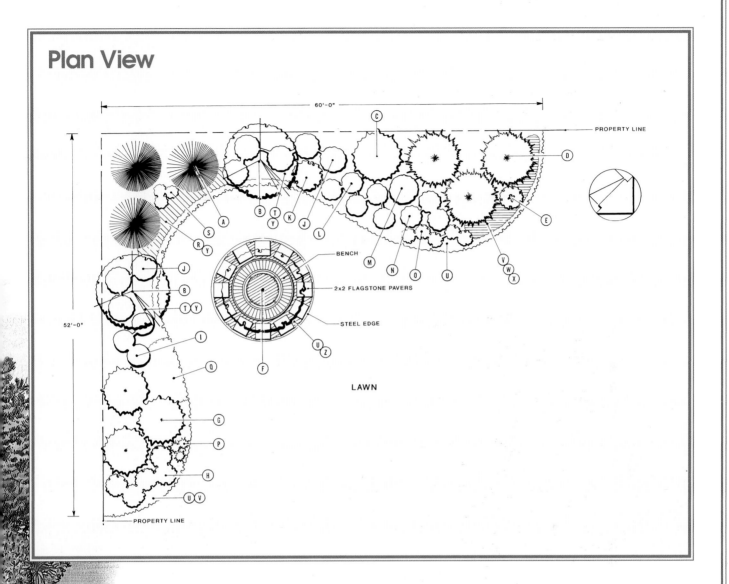

60'-0"

52'-0"

PROPERTY LINE

PROPERTY LINE

BENCH

2x2 FLAGSTONE PAVERS

STEEL EDGE

LAWN

plan# **HPT94042**

SHOWN IN SPRING
DESIGN BY JIM MORGAN

SEE PAGE 153 TO ORDER OUR
COMPREHENSIVE BLUEPRINT
PACKAGE, INCLUDING A REGIONAL-
IZED PLANT AND MATERIALS LIST AND
OTHER INVALUABLE INFORMATION TO
HELP YOU CREATE THIS LANDSCAPE.

Here, a dense planting of assorted
evergreens, set off by a changing
show of flowering deciduous trees
and shrubs, creates privacy from a
neighboring property and also
effectively muffles noise.

CHAPTER 10

Child's Play

Yards with Fun in Mind

Install a landscape filled with a variety of activities and natural beauty, and your kids will be begging to go outside and play. With the right plantings and design elements, you'll be able to create a yard that both kids and adults can enjoy.

Turn loose a couple of little boys or girls on an acre of land with lawn, an old tree, a stand of tall grass, a pile of scrap lumber, and a regulation jungle gym, and where will you find the kids playing? Chances are, given time, they'll check out a little bit of everything. Kids are inventive and easily bored, so they will take over any space available to them. You'll want to plan for plenty of options to keep them busy—and enjoying the outdoors instead of sitting on the couch.

It takes more than a swing set to keep children occupied for any extended period of time. Set aside a corner of a 60-foot-lot, label it for children only, and you've acknowledged your kids' right to have their own space—but know that they won't be confined to it. If you're wise you'll realize that your children will use not just the sandbox, swing set, and basketball hoop, but the entire yard as a playground, and you'll design the yard accordingly. The designs in this chapter are perfect examples of yards where both children and parents will feel at home.

The first step in planning a yard for children is to take time to think about your kids' particular styles of play. What are their favorite toys, games, and activi-

RIGHT: Incorporating arts and crafts into your yard with playful decor is sure to delight young and old.

Comprehensive blueprint packages are available for each of the designs in this chapter. Professionally designed and prepared with precise attention to detail, these easy-to-follow plans include:
- a precise plot plan
- regionalized plant and materials lists
- a plant size and description guide
- installation and maintenance information

These plans will help you or your contractor achieve professional results, adding beauty and value to your property for years. Turn to page 153 for ordering information.

ties? Are your children physically active types who are likely to need lots of space to run, jump, and ride, or are they more contemplative and happy to play in one spot for hours? Do they pay attention to boundaries, or do they often forget what they are doing in the excitement of play?

Make a list of your backyard requirements and then consider how you can accomplish them in your particular site. And don't neglect to ask your children what they would like in a play yard. They'll be excited to be involved in the process, and you may make some important discoveries. Perhaps they're more interested in having a place to dig than a place to swing. Maybe one child dreams of having a playhouse or a tree house, while the other would love a hopscotch court.

As the designs in this chapter show, your backyard doesn't have to be complicated to succeed for both you and your children. Focus on the basic elements of your landscape—the placement of the patio, lawn, trees, shrubs, and special play equipment. You can always elaborate the details later.

CREATING GREAT PLAY AREAS

Children are easy to please, so you don't need to invest in an expensive playhouse or other structure if the cost is beyond your budget. A hiding place, even if it's carved out of a shrubbery border, can be a special place for a child. An overhanging branch, an old tree stump, or a low wall can provide enough camouflage or protection to become the basis for an imaginary fort or playhouse.

A sturdy, low-branched tree can be a great resource for a child. Besides providing an excellent place for climbing, the tree can serve as a support for a swing, rope ladder, or tree house.

When you're figuring out your family's requirements, keep the following in mind:

■ Children have wonderful imaginations. Encourage them by providing interesting nooks and crannies for hiding places. Create trails through the shrubbery and yard for exploring and make-believe games.

■ Kids love to climb. If you don't have a good climbing tree in your yard, consider providing some type of structure for that purpose. If you don't, kids might find something less safe to scale.

■ Children need both hard and soft surfaces to play on. A lawn is an ideal place for tumbling and roughhousing; pavement works better for bike riding and basketball.

■ Children like to have something of their very own. To get kids interested in gardening and science, give them a small garden spot of their own and help them grow the fruits and vegetables they like to eat, like in our Child's Garden of Fun plan (page 136).

■ Kids play exuberantly. Design your landscape with tough plants, and protect your own garden space from balls and bike wheels with fencing or hedges.

■ Children grow up before you know it. Plan ahead for when kids are older and won't need a yard for active playing. Locate the sandbox where it can be easily transformed into an attractive raised strawberry bed, or construct the kids' vegetable garden where a cut-flower bed could replace it in time.

■ Youngsters need supervision. Design a children's yard so that all play areas can be seen from indoors and from the patio or terrace. Fences with locked gates provide additional security.

PLANNING FOR SAFE PLAY

Much like children's tastes, the safety requirements of play areas can change depending on their age. When your children are young, you'll have to design a play space that won't cause skinned knees and is resistant to the wear and tear of active feet. Once they are older and more independent, your kids may become interested in group sports and you can remake the yard, adding a badminton court or a hard-surfaced shuffleboard court where the entire family can play together.

The ultimate paving for active children is grass, and a patch of lawn is often first on a parent's backyard landscaping list. No other surface feels as soft and cool underfoot or looks as attractive. And a lawn doesn't need to be large to be useful. In small backyards, and in areas where water is in short supply, 600 to 800 square feet is more than enough to provide a soft, resilient surface for your kids to play on. Adding a berm, or raised area,

to an otherwise flat lawn provides a fun place for kids to turn somersaults and build fortresses.

For riding bikes, pulling wagons, or playing hopscotch, hard paving is essential. A paved surface in the backyard like concrete, brick, stone, or wood can help keep kids safe by keeping them out of the street. Pea gravel, decomposed granite, and sand are other good options. Poured concrete—the best surface for wheeled toys—can be finished in different textures to make it more attractive. Try to select a material and color that works well with your house and the surroundings.

The tactile pleasure of sand never quite leaves us, and children glory in it. Easily added to any backyard, a sandbox can be as simple as a rubber tire or an inflated play pool filled with sharp builder's sand. (Avoid beach sand, which is too salty and can affect the pH of your soil.) A large sandbox located beneath a play structure provides a great place for digging and building, while reducing the risk of injury from falls and jumps. To keep sand from getting muddy, you should separate it from the soil beneath with landscape fabric. A cover for a sandbox—made from a plastic sheet, canvas, wood, or acrylic—will keep rain, pets, and debris out.

ENTICING PLAY STRUCTURES

All kinds of play structures—from the traditional metal swing set to elaborate wood structures that include swings, turrets, and monkey bars—are available ready-made. Our Backyard Playground plan (page 134) is a perfect example of an enticing jungle gym. The big advantage of a prefabricated structure is that the engineering has been done to ensure its sturdiness and safety.

You can also make a simple swing from a tree branch with nothing more than a strong rope with a knot at the end and a board for a seat. A tree house can consist of a sturdy platform with a ladder and a railing. ■

BACKYARD PLAYGROUND

plan# HPT94043

**SHOWN IN SUMMER
DESIGN BY MICHAEL J. OPISSO**

SEE PAGE 153 TO ORDER OUR COMPREHENSIVE BLUEPRINT PACKAGE, INCLUDING A REGIONALIZED PLANT AND MATERIALS LIST AND OTHER INVALUABLE INFORMATION TO HELP YOU CREATE THIS LANDSCAPE.

Here is a special backyard designed for both children and adults. The yard offers youngsters their own place to escape into a world of imagination and discovery without compromising the attractiveness of a garden setting.

Plan View

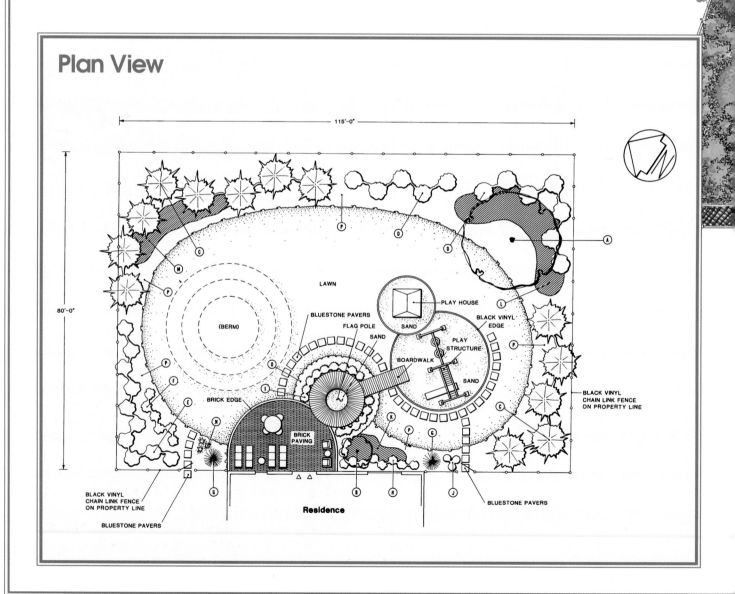

115'-0"

80'-0"

LAWN

(BERM)

BLUESTONE PAVERS

FLAG POLE

SAND

BRICK EDGE

PLAY HOUSE

SAND

BLACK VINYL EDGE

PLAY STRUCTURE

BOARDWALK

SAND

BLACK VINYL CHAIN LINK FENCE ON PROPERTY LINE

BRICK PAVING

BLACK VINYL CHAIN LINK FENCE ON PROPERTY LINE

BLUESTONE PAVERS

BLUESTONE PAVERS

Residence

If there's one thing that can be said about children's play areas, it's that their function usually far outweighs their attractiveness. However, this backyard design presents an excellent solution to a functional children's play yard that is still pleasing to look at. The backyard includes all the fun elements a child would love. On one side of the yard are grouped a play structure for climbing and swinging, a playhouse, and a sandbox enclosed in a low boardwalk. A play mound—a perfect place for running, leaping, and holding fort—rises from the lawn on the other side of the yard.

These play areas are integrated into the landscape by their circular form, which is repeated in the sandbox, play mound, boardwalk, and the sand areas under the playhouse and play structure. The curved brick patio and planting border carry through the circular theme. The stepping stones leading to the play areas also follow a circular path—a playful pattern that invites a child to "follow the yellow brick road."

From the house and patio, the views of both the garden and the play areas are unobstructed, affording constant adult supervision from both indoors and out. The border surrounding the yard creates a private setting that offers a changing show of flowers from the masses of shrubs and perennials. Beyond the play structure, a large tree shades the area, providing landscape interest, and perhaps even a place for adventurous young feet to climb.

When the children are grown, this design can be adapted as a playground for older folk by removing the playhouse and play structure, and planting lawn, or a flower or vegetable garden.

A CHILD'S GARDEN OF FUN

Young gardeners will thrive in this backyard, which is specially designed to entice a child into horticulture with a circular vegetable garden and a barn-and-silo playhouse or toolshed. The stepping-stones in the garden make a perfect spot for hopscotch, and the swing set, sandbox, and lawn provide other places to romp.

Vegetables grow just as well in beds as in rows, and the circular bed used here better suits a child's sense of necessary disorder. Surrounded by a gravel path and crisscrossed by pathways, the garden presents four individual easy-care beds that can be planted with several types of vegetables. Begin with your child's favorites in order to create enthusiasm for gar-

dening. Then add a few new ones to encourage investigation. Eating a vine-ripened tomato grown personally by the child may be enough to convert a typical play-obsessed ten-year-old into a lifelong gardener.

Parents will like this backyard design, too. It combines a permanent structure of easy-care trees, shrubs, and perennials, which produce a beautiful color display spring through fall, and a handsome brick patio for relaxing and entertaining. The circular shape of the vegetable bed, which can be turned into a pretty herb or flower bed, echoes the curves of the lawn, making it an attractive, yet functional, design element. For safety's sake, the entire backyard is open and visible from the patio and has only one gate.

Plan View

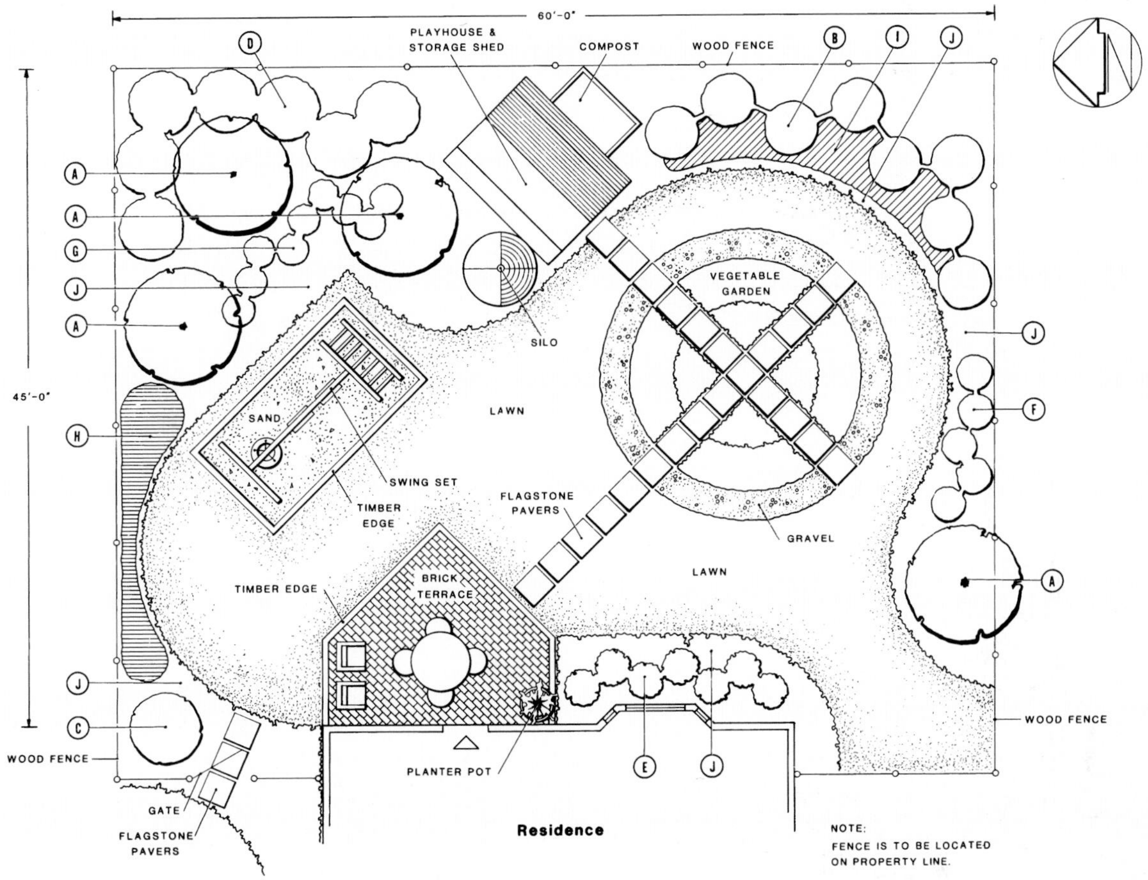

Plan view labels:
- 60'-0"
- 45'-0"
- D
- PLAYHOUSE & STORAGE SHED
- COMPOST
- WOOD FENCE
- B
- I
- J
- A
- A
- G
- J
- A
- H
- VEGETABLE GARDEN
- SILO
- LAWN
- SAND
- SWING SET
- TIMBER EDGE
- FLAGSTONE PAVERS
- J
- F
- TIMBER EDGE
- BRICK TERRACE
- GRAVEL
- LAWN
- A
- J
- C
- PLANTER POT
- E
- J
- WOOD FENCE
- WOOD FENCE
- GATE
- FLAGSTONE PAVERS
- Residence
- NOTE: FENCE IS TO BE LOCATED ON PROPERTY LINE.

A child can skip right along the stepping stones to tend a personal vegetable garden in this cleverly designed backyard. With a barn-and-silo playhouse and compost bin adjacent to the garden, your child can exercise imagination in creative play while helping with the chores and learning about recycling.

plan # HPT94044

SHOWN IN SUMMER
DESIGN BY MICHAEL J. OPISSO

SEE PAGE 153 TO ORDER OUR COMPREHENSIVE BLUEPRINT PACKAGE, INCLUDING A REGIONALIZED PLANT AND MATERIALS LIST AND OTHER INVALUABLE INFORMATION TO HELP YOU CREATE THIS LANDSCAPE.

HELLO, SPORTS FANS!

plan# HPT94045

**SHOWN IN SUMMER
DESIGN BY MICHAEL J. OPISSO**

SEE PAGE 153 TO ORDER OUR
COMPREHENSIVE BLUEPRINT
PACKAGE, INCLUDING A REGIONAL-
IZED PLANT AND MATERIALS LIST AND
OTHER INVALUABLE INFORMATION TO
HELP YOU CREATE THIS LANDSCAPE.

The ideal backyard for a sports-
minded family, this design features
three permanent playing fields to
provide children and adults alike
with plenty of play options.

Plan View

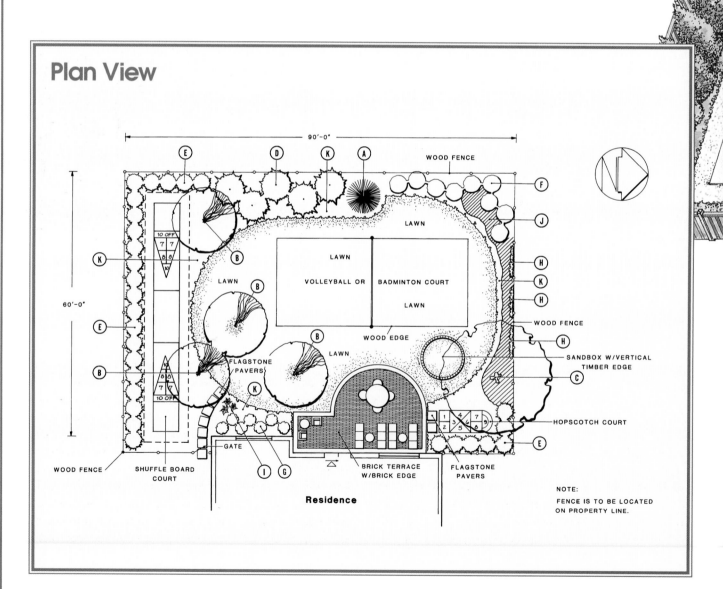

If your family is the energetic kind that never stops moving, this backyard plan provides the perfect solution for soaking up all their enthusiasm. Three play courts are permanently installed: shuffleboard, badminton, and hopscotch. All are discreetly integrated with other elements of the landscape to create a beautiful, but functional, backyard.

In the center of the lawn, the outer dimensions of a volleyball or badminton court are marked inconspicuously with landscape timbers laid on edge and flush with the ground. Set this way, they don't interfere with mowing or cause anyone to trip, yet they remain as clear markers. You can make bolder, temporary official court lines in the lawn with garden lime, gypsum, or flour—none of which will harm the grass.

The shuffleboard and hopscotch courts in the perimeter of the yard are made from poured concrete. Both are partially hidden behind shrubs and trees and are surrounded by an evergreen groundcover to soften their hard edges. Younger children will delight in the circular timber-edged sandbox, which can be turned into a flower or strawberry bed when the kids outgrow sand-castle and fort building.

The brick patio, attractively curved to mimic the shape of the lawn, allows plenty of space for adults to relax in the sun, dine outdoors, and enjoy a commanding view of all the sports action.

SWING IN THE SUNSHINE

plan# HPT94046

SHOWN IN SPRING
DESIGN BY DAMON SCOTT

SEE PAGE 153 TO ORDER OUR COMPREHENSIVE BLUEPRINT PACKAGE, INCLUDING A REGIONALIZED PLANT AND MATERIALS LIST AND OTHER INVALUABLE INFORMATION TO HELP YOU CREATE THIS LANDSCAPE.

Could any child resist this wonderful backyard? Circular sand pits—designed for both play and safety—combined with a fabulous play structure makes this backyard as exciting as the local park.

Plan View

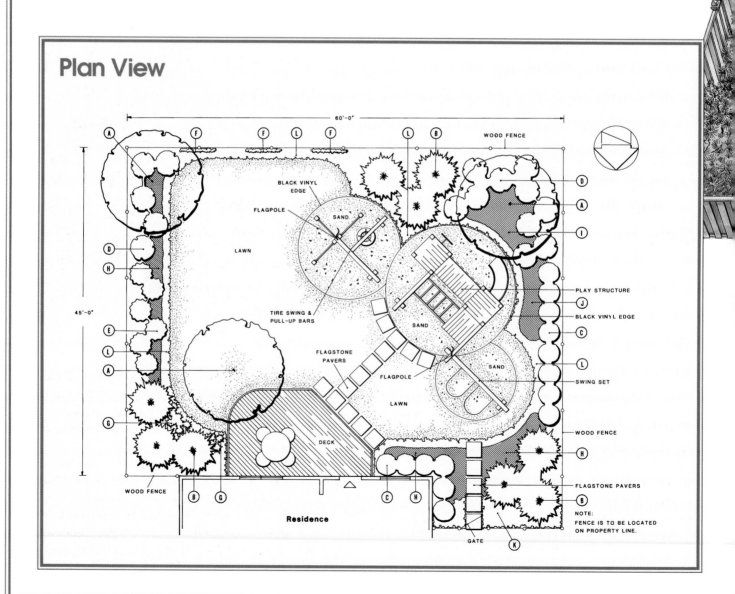

Your young, active children and their friends will enjoy hours of engaging play in this wonderful backyard. The elaborate play structures, which are designed to exercise every growing muscle a kid has to develop, features many different elements—a hanging tire, pull-up bars, slides, swings, and rings, as well as platforms for game playing. With so many choices, a child's short attention span is sure to be accommodated. Besides the obvious play structures, the yard includes secret hiding places nestled behind the shrubs and under the trees in the yard's corners—these will lure any child in need of a quiet, contemplative moment.

The repeating circles beneath the play structure create the landscape's main design feature. These are actually giant sand pits. They're bordered by easy-to-install vinyl strips that keep the sand from spilling onto the lawn. With the play structures set off center of the yard, plenty of lawn area remains for running games and visual beauty.

Although a wood fence at the property line borders the yard for security reasons, the densely planted trees and shrubs enhance the sense of privacy and enclosure, while providing colorful flowers and softening greenery. The wood deck, accessible from the house through sliding glass doors, balances the visual weight of the play structure. The deck's diagonal lines and squared-off shape make a happy contrast with the circular sand pits.

LINKSIDE STREAM

The main feature of this design is the large putting green with room for any foursome. The sand bunker allows for further honing of your skills. The "bear claw" tot putting green is a perfect place for little ones to learn the game, or it could function as a tee area, making this a great all-around "practice facility."

A multi-tiered deck is perfect for both outdoor parties and private moonlight relaxation. Inviting walkways lead you toward the gardens (designed to attract butterflies) and an arboretum, and then to an art studio for creative endeavors

and solitude. Another path links the studio to the elevated retreat, a place to relax in the garden swing while viewing the entire grounds.

The tranquil sounds of the ponds set the stage for meditation, even as boulders contribute a sense of scale found in the wild. Linking the two halves of the grounds, a bridge takes you by a waterfall and moves you from the tranquil side toward the active.

Final touches to the plan include built-in seating around the deck, a deluxe barbecue and trellises and arbors anchoring the home to the site.

Plan View

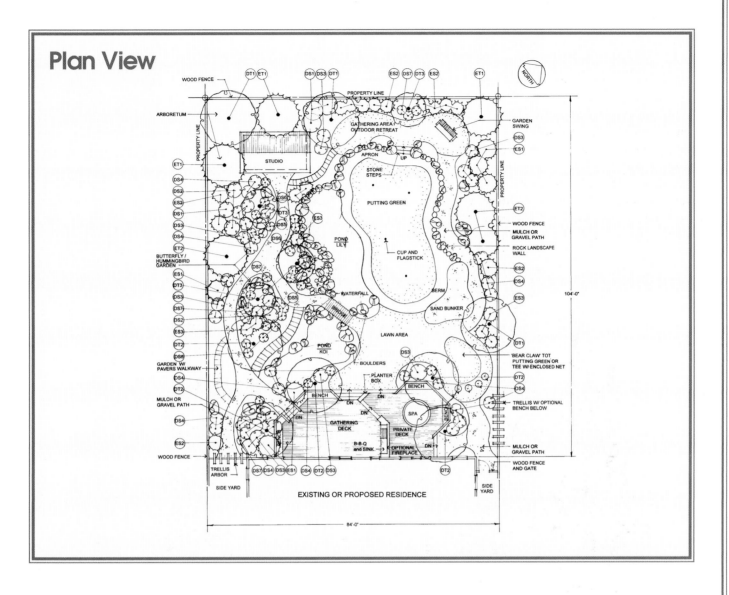

plan# **HPT94047**

Designed for an estate or a large suburban parcel, this plan is a hefty 8,736 square feet. Offering lush surroundings and spaces for both social activities and solitude, this backyard is a gardener's delight and a golfer's paradise.

SHOWN IN SUMMER
DESIGN BY PAR 3 GOLF

SEE PAGE 153 TO ORDER OUR COMPREHENSIVE BLUEPRINT PACKAGE, INCLUDING A REGIONALIZED PLANT AND MATERIALS LIST AND OTHER INVALUABLE INFORMATION TO HELP YOU CREATE THIS LANDSCAPE.

CHAPTER 11

Installing Your Landscape
Make Your Dream a Reality

Once you've found your dream landscape, we can help you make it work in your yard. Whether you're a do-it-yourselfer or plan to hire a contractor, the following pages will help you adapt your plan to your specific setting and install it to give you years of enjoyment.

Regionalized plant lists and essential design elements are available for all the landscapes in this book (see page 153 for ordering information). But because every yard is unique, you may need to adapt the plan you choose to fit your site.

The designs in this book were created to fit easily into a variety of typical property sizes and shapes. If your property varies from these, however, that shouldn't be a major problem; you can easily adapt the plans to a larger, smaller, or differently shaped site.

Once you've purchased a landscape plan, start by placing your plan on an existing survey of your property. You can do this—even if you aren't an artist—with a few simple tools. You'll need tracing paper, pencils, an eraser, a scale ruler, and several large sheets of graph paper. Graph paper comes in various sizes,

but 18-by-24-inch sheets are the most useful, because they're the same size as the blueprints for the plans in this book. Although a scale ruler isn't essential, you'll find that it makes measuring to scale much quicker. To make your plan as legible as possible, you may also want to have on hand a T-square, a template of landscape symbols, and a compass.

You'll also need an accurate drawing of your existing property. The best way to start is with your property survey—or an accurate measurement of your space that you draw yourself. Draw your property's layout using a convenient scale—usually 1 inch of drawing representing either 4 feet (¼ scale) or 8 feet (⅛ scale) of property. The blueprints of the plans in this book

RIGHT: An older tree and a stone wall lend a timeless quality to this backyard garden.

use one of those two scales.

On tracing paper, redraw the portion of your property where you intend to install the landscape, enlarging it to fit the chosen scale. Then add all existing and permanent features that you want to keep, such as pathways, a patio or deck, and walls. Next, add in all existing trees, shrubs, and garden areas that you want to keep.

If your house is on the plot plan, note the locations of all doors and windows. This will help you site a garden to take advantage of a view or traffic pattern. Don't guess at the dimensions: use a 50- or 100-foot tape measure and work as precisely as you can. Finally, using a directional arrow, mark which way is north. Once your drawing is complete, photocopy it so that you can experiment on the copies and keep the original safe and clean.

Lay the tracing-paper copy of your existing landscape over the blueprint of the plan, moving it around until you find the best fit. Making adjustments to the design at this point is easy:

■ Place another piece of tracing paper on the top of the two drawings (use small pieces of tape to keep the sheets aligned), and trace the permanent features onto the new sheet of paper.

■ Undo the tape and remove the tracing of the existing plot plan. Shift the new paper over the design, tracing its prominent features in slightly different locations.

ADJUSTING FOR LOT SIZE OR SHAPE

If you expand the perimeter of the original design, don't simply add more space between the designated number of plants. You'll want to maintain the right amount of space between individual plants, and not make the garden appear too sparse.

To adjust the design to a larger site, simply plant the design according to the plan and increase the number of plants in each group (or drift) using the indicated

LEFT: Containerized plants can help tie an outdoor dining area to the landscape that surrounds it.

spacing. Adding between three and five plants to a drift is fine, but adding more may change the integrity and scale of the design. If you need to fill a much larger space, try repeating a drift or several drifts of plants from one part of the garden, rather than enlarging a single grouping into a huge mass. Repeating drifts in a garden bed or border creates a pleasing sense of rhythm as your eye travels along and recognizes a pattern.

To adjust a design to a smaller piece of property, take out several plants from each group of plants along the length or width of the design. This reduces the overall scale of the landscape without destroying the original design.

ADJUSTING PLANS TO A SLOPE

Most of the designs in this book were created for relatively flat pieces of property or for lots with a slight slope. If your property is more sloped, you can adjust many of these plans to fit, either by regrading or by adding retaining walls. A change of grade involves more than just aesthetics; you may require an engineer or licensed contractor to ensure that changing the grade doesn't create drainage problems.

Professional designers often use retaining walls to create multiple flat levels out of steeply sloped ground. The walls are not only functional, but can be attractive. You can build them out of landscape timbers, bricks, stones, or another material that matches your home's architecture. When planning a retaining wall, include drainage pipes at the base to prevent water buildup behind the wall.

Almost every property – even if it seems perfectly flat – has some grade (slope) or dips and rises. (The "grade" of a property shouldn't be confused with "grading," which is the term used to describe changing the existing slope.) You should assess the variations in grade on your property and consider any necessary or desired grade changes before finalizing the landscape design.

Whether your grading change calls for simply flattening a small area for a patio, or a major change like grading an entire lawn, you want to carefully consider the consequences before you begin work. Before attempting any major changes in grade, or before paving large areas near the house, consult a professional to ensure that your plan won't cause drainage problems. He or she can help determine whether drainage tiles or pipes need to be installed, or how to change the grade to avoid problems.

Take care not to change the grade around the drip line of a large tree, because this can either expose or bury the roots, eventually killing the tree. If you need to raise the grade around a tree, construct a well around it to avoid burying the roots.

It's best to grade your property so that water drains away from structures and doesn't collect in beds, borders, and paved areas. Proper grading can also prevent water from collecting in a basement after heavy rain and eliminates low areas where water and snow collect instead of draining away properly.

Paved areas should maintain a minimum pitch of ⅛ inch per foot, but ½ inch is better. A patio that's located next to the house should slope slightly away from the structure. If the patio is located in a lower part of the landscape, where water can't run off because of a wall or higher ground surrounding it, you'll need drains and drainage pipes to channel water away. Consult a landscape contractor to ensure a practical and economical solution. You may also need to check with utility companies to determine the location of any underground pipes and cables.

INSTALLING YOUR GARDEN DESIGN

Whether you plant a garden and construct walkways, a deck, or a patio yourself, or hire a contractor to do all or part of the work, check local building codes before you begin any extensive landscaping.

RIGHT: A well-placed arbor and bench becomes a focal point in your landscape, as well as a secluded place to relax.

Many communities have building codes that may affect the height of shrubs, walls, and fences at the property line, especially along the street. Permanent structures and home improvements, such as decks, patios, and retaining walls, may require a permit.

Communities often require proof of proper engineering and, in most cases, demand that such structures be a certain distance from the property line. Swimming pools almost always require a fence or enclosure to prevent small children from accidentally wandering into the area; a garden pool may also need a fence if it is more than 18 inches deep. It's your responsibility to find out which regulations apply to landscaping in your community.

Before you begin planting, it's important to prepare the soil thoroughly to create a healthy environment for your plants. The best way to start is with a soil test, conducted by your local county extension service or a private soil-testing laboratory. Along with the results, you'll get detailed recommendations on how to improve your soil. These will most likely include adding organic matter, such as composted bark or sawdust. Spread 2 or 3 inches of the organic material over the soil where you'll be planting and till it in. Additional fertilizer, and perhaps lime or sulfur to adjust the soil pH, may also be recommended.

You may need to remove lawn to make room for your landscape plan. You can strip the lawn away just below the roots with a spade, or you can rent a power sod cutter. Sod that's stripped off can be saved and transplanted where it's needed, or you can use it as fill or add it to a compost pile. Lawns can also be killed with an herbicide such as glyphosate, but be careful not to spray the chemical on desirable plants, or you'll kill them. Finally, you can smother an existing lawn under a deep layer of mulch.

Once you've cleared the area to be landscaped, use a measuring tape to mark the

LEFT: Bright flowers provide privacy for sunbathers and help separate the lawn from the pool area.

outlines of the new garden. You can use wood or metal stakes and run strings between them to show clearly where everything will be located. A garden hose or a clothesline works well to outline flower beds and borders. A sprinkling of garden lime or flour also works well to trace outlines and mark planting locations. You'll want to place markers to indicate areas of major construction, such as a deck, pool, or walkway, and to mark the sites of large trees.

When you are ready to plant, set out all the plants intended for the garden according to the planting plan, but don't remove them from their containers. Study their locations from several angles and make adjustments as needed before you plant. Then mark their holes with lime or flour and dig. Remove each plant from its container one at a time, just before planting, to prevent the roots from drying out.

HIRING A LANDSCAPE CONTRACTOR

The virtue of the plans offered in this book is that you can enjoy the benefits of a professional design without paying what you would for custom landscaping. Handy do-it-yourselfers can easily manage the variety of tasks required to install a bed or border. Others may wish to hire a landscape contractor to do some or all of the installation.

Ask your friends and neighbors for recommendations for a contractor, but be sure to see examples of their work and check their references before you hire anyone. Once you've decided on an individual, write out a contract that specifies work and payment schedules.

When your landscape is finished, the property will have a beautiful look that you and your family will enjoy for years to come. The new garden will improve your outdoor environment the day it's completed, and the initial investment will more than pay for itself by adding to the value of your home. ∎

BELOW: These bright purple hydrangea serve as the perfect complement to the home's weathered wood siding.

THE LANDSCAPE BLUEPRINT PACKAGE

THE LANDSCAPE BLUEPRINT PACKAGE AVAILABLE FROM HOME PLANNERS

includes all the necessary information you need to lay out and install the landscape design of your choice. Professionally designed and prepared with attention to detail, these clear, easy-to-follow plans offer everything from a precise plot plan and regionalized plant and materials list to helpful sheets on installing your landscape and determining the mature size of your plants. These plans will help you achieve professional-looking results, adding value and enjoyment to your property for years to come.

Each set of blueprints is a full 18"x 24" in size with clear, complete instructions and easy-to-read type. Consisting of six detailed sheets, these plans show how all plants and materials are put together to form an exciting landscape for your home.

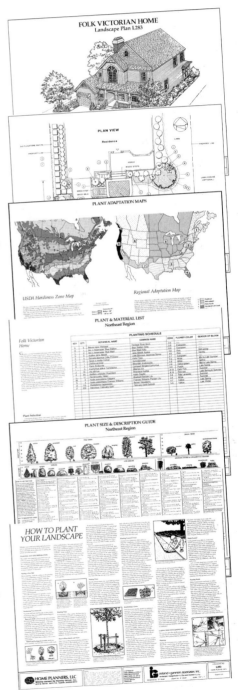

FRONTAL SHEET
This artist's line sketch shows a typical house (if applicable) and all the elements of the finished landscape when plants are at or near maturity. This will give you a visual image or "picture" of the design and what you might expect your property to look like when fully landscaped.

PLAN VIEW
This is an aerial view of the property showing the exact placement of all landscape elements, including symbols and call-outs for flowers, shrubs, groundcovers, walkways, walls, gates and other garden amenities. This sheet is the key to the design and shows you the contour, spacing, flow and balance of all the elements in the design, as well as providing an exact "map" for laying out your property.

ZONE MAPS
These two informative maps offer detailed information to help you better select and judge the performance of your plants. Map One is a United States Department of Agriculture Hardiness Zone Map that shows the average low temperatures by zones in various parts of the United States and Canada. The "Zone" listing for plants on Sheet 3 of your Plant and Materials List is keyed to this map. Map Two is a Regional Adaptation Map, which takes into account other factors beyond low temperatures, such as rainfall, humidity, extremes of temperature, and soil acidity or alkalinity. Both maps are key to plant adaptability and are used for the selection of landscape plants for your plans.

REGIONALIZED PLANT & MATERIALS LIST
Keyed to the Plan View sheet, this page lists all of the plants and materials necessary to execute the design. It gives the quantity, botanical name, common name, flower color, season of bloom and hardiness zones for each plant specified. This becomes your "shopping list" for dealing with contractors or buying the plants and materials yourself. Most importantly, the plants shown on this page have been chosen by a team of professional horticulturalists for their adaptability, availability and performance in your specific part of the country.

PLANT SIZE & DESCRIPTION GUIDE
Because you may have trouble visualizing certain plants, this handy regionalized guide provides a scale and silhouettes to help you determine the final height and shape of various trees and shrubs in your landscape plan. It also provides a quick means of choosing alternate plants appropriate to your region in case you do not wish to install a certain tree or shrub, or if you cannot find the plant at local nurseries.

PLANTING & MAINTAINING YOUR LANDSCAPE
This valuable sheet gives handy information and illustrations on purchasing plant materials, preparing your site and caring for your landscape after installation. Includes quick, helpful advice on planting trees, shrubs and groundcovers, staking trees, establishing a lawn, watering, weed control and pruning.

LANDSCAPE REGIONS

REGIONAL ORDER MAP

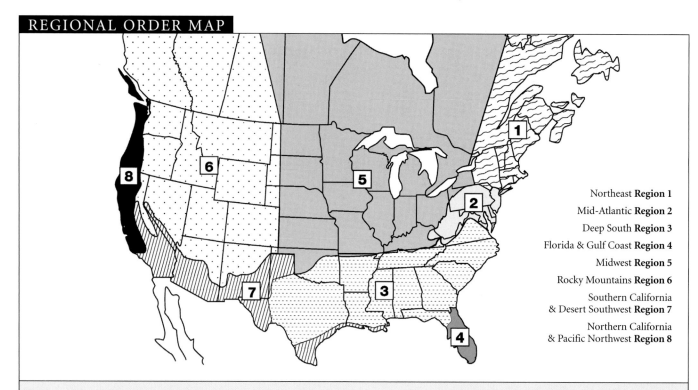

Northeast **Region 1**

Mid-Atlantic **Region 2**

Deep South **Region 3**

Florida & Gulf Coast **Region 4**

Midwest **Region 5**

Rocky Mountains **Region 6**

Southern California
& Desert Southwest **Region 7**

Northern California
& Pacific Northwest **Region 8**

To use the Index, refer to the design number listed in numerical order (a helpful page reference is also given). Note the price tier and refer to the Blueprint Price Schedule for the cost of one, four or eight sets of blueprints or the cost of a reproducible drawing. Additional prices are shown for identical and reverse blueprint sets.

TO ORDER, Call toll free 1-800-521-6797 for current pricing and availability prior to mailing the order form.
FAX: 1-800-224-6699 or 520-544-3086.

PICTURE CREDITS

Page 1: Julie Maris/Semel.

Page 3: Karen Bussolini (top left); Rick Weatherbee (middle left); Bill Geddes (lower left); Tria Giovan (right).

Page 5: Photo courtesy of Netherlands Flower Bulb Information Center.

Page 6: Photo courtesy of Netherlands Flower Bulb Information Center.

Page 7: Art by Gordon Morrison.

Page 8: Photo courtesy of Netherlands Flower Bulb Information Center (top); Monrovia (bottom).

Page 9: Art by Gordon Morrison.

Page 10: Courtesy of Green City Designs.com.

Page 11: Art by Gordon Morrison; Photo courtesy of Netherlands Flower Bulb Information Center.

Page 12: Photo courtesy of Netherlands

Flower Bulb Information Center.

Page 13: Photo by judywhite/gardenphotos.com; Art by Gordon Morrison.

Page 15: Mark Samu.

Page 16: Jessie Walker.

Page 17: Mark Samu; Inset photo by Mark Lohman.

Page 33: Rick Weatherbee.

Page 34: Photo courtesy of Netherlands Flower Bulb Information Center.

Page 35: judywhite/gardenphotos.com.

Page 47: judywhite/gardenphotos.com.

Page 48: judywhite/gardenphotos.com.

Page 49: Linda Bellamy.

Page 61: Rick Weatherbee.

Page 62: judywhite/gardenphotos.com.

Page 75: Rick Weatherbee.

Page 76: Mark Samu.

Page 77: Karen Bussolini.

Page 89: Mark Samu.

Page 90: Mark Samu.

Page 103: Julie Maris/Semel.

Page 104: Karen Bussolini.

Page 105: Tria Giovan.

Page 117: Mark Lohman.

Page 118: Rick Weatherbee.

Page 119: Tria Giovan.

Page 131: Bill Geddes.

Page 132: judywhite/gardenphotos.com.

Page 145: Bill Geddes.

Page 146: Mark Samu.

Page 149: Photo by Ernest Braun, courtesy of California Redwood Association.

Page 151: Julie Maris/Semel.

Page 152: Sam Gray.

Page 160: Photo courtesy of Netherlands Flower Bulb Information Center.

PRICE SCHEDULE & INDEX

TO ORDER YOUR PLANS,

simply find the Plan Number of the design of your choice in the Plans Index below. Consult the Price Schedule to determine the price of your plans, choosing the 1-set package for Landscape Plans and any additional or reverse sets you desire. If ordering Landscape Plans, make sure your Plant and Materials List contains the best selection for your area by referring to the Regional Order Map below and specifying the region in which you will be building. Fill out the Order Coupon and mail it to us for prompt fulfillment or call our Toll-Free Order Hotline for even faster service.

BLUEPRINT PRICE SCHEDULE

TIERS	1-SET STUDY PACKAGE	4-SET BUILDING PACKAGE	8-SET BUILDING PACKAGE	1-SET REPRODUCIBLE*
P1	$20	$50	$90	$140
P2	$40	$70	$110	$160
P3	$70	$100	$140	$190
P4	$100	$130	$170	$220
P5	$140	$170	$210	$270
P6	$180	$210	$250	$310

Requires a fax number

IMPORTANT NOTES
• The 1-set study package is marked "not for construction."
• Prices for 4- or 8-set Building Packages honored only at time of original order.
• Additional identical blueprints may be purchased within 60 days of original order.

OPTIONS FOR PLANS IN TIERS P1–P6
Additional Identical Blueprints in same order for "P1–P6" price plans ....**$10 per set**
Reverse Blueprints (mirror image) for "P1–P6" price plans...**$10 fee per order**
1 Set of Deck or Gazebo Construction Details ....**$14.95 each**
Deck or Gazebo Construction Package..**add $10 to Building Package price**
(includes 1 set of "P1–P6" plans, plus 1 set Standard Gazebo Construction Details)

PLAN INDEX

Before filling out the order form, please call us on our Toll-Free Blueprint Hotline 1-800-521-6797. You may want to learn more about our services and products. Here's some information you will find helpful.

OUR EXCHANGE POLICY

With the exception of reproducible plan orders, we will exchange your entire first order for an equal or greater number of blueprints within our plan collection within 90 days of the original order. The entire content of your original order must be returned before an exchange will be processed. Please call our customer service department for your return authorization number and shipping instructions. If the returned blueprints look used, redlined or copied, we will not honor your exchange. Fees for exchanging your blueprints are as follows: 20% of the amount of the original order...plus the difference in cost if exchanging for a design in a higher price bracket or less the difference in cost if exchanging for a design in a lower price bracket. **(Reproducible blueprints are not exchangeable or refundable.)** Please call for current postage and handling prices. Shipping and handling charges are not refundable. Please call our customer service department for your return authorization number and shipping instructions.

ABOUT REPRODUCIBLES

When purchasing a reproducible you may be required to furnish a fax number. The designer will fax documents that you must sign and return to them before shipping will take place.

ABOUT REVERSE BLUEPRINTS

Although lettering and dimensions will appear backward, reverses will be a useful aid if you decide to flop the plan. See Price Schedule and Plans Index for pricing.

REVISING, MODIFYING AND CUSTOMIZING PLANS

Like many homeowners who buy these plans, you and your builder, architect or engineer may want to make changes to them. We recommend purchase of a reproducible plan for any changes made by your builder, licensed architect or engineer. As set forth below, we cannot assume any responsibility for blueprints which have been changed, whether by you, your builder or by professionals selected by you or referred to you by us, because such individuals are outside our supervision and control.

ARCHITECTURAL AND ENGINEERING SEALS

Some cities and states are now requiring that a licensed architect or engineer review and "seal" a blueprint, or officially approve it, prior to construction due to concerns over energy costs, safety and other factors. Prior to application for a building permit or the start of actual construction, we strongly advise that you consult your local building official who can tell you if such a review is required.

ABOUT THE DESIGNS

The architects and designers whose work appears in this publication are among America's leading residential designers. Each plan was designed to meet the requirements of a nationally recognized model building code in effect at the time and place the plan was drawn. Because national building codes change from time to time, plans may not comply with any such code at the time they are sold to a customer. In addition, building officials may not accept these plans as final construction documents of record as the plans may need to be modified and additional drawings and details added to suit local conditions and requirements. We strongly advise that purchasers consult a licensed architect or engineer, and their local building official, before starting any construction related to these plans.

LOCAL BUILDING CODES AND ZONING REQUIREMENTS

At the time of creation, our plans are drawn to specifications published by the Building Officials and Code Administrators (BOCA) International, Inc.; the Southern Building Code Congress (SBCCI) International, Inc.; the International Conference of Building Officials (ICBO); or the Council of American Building Officials (CABO). Our plans are designed to meet or exceed national building standards. Because of the great differences in geography and climate throughout the United States and Canada, each state, county and municipality has its own building codes, zone requirements, ordinances and building regulations. Your plan may need to be modified to comply with local requirements regarding snow loads, energy codes, soil and seismic conditions and a wide range of other matters. In addition, you may need to obtain permits or inspections from local governments before and in the course of construction. Prior to using blueprints ordered from us, we strongly advise that you consult a licensed architect or engineer—and speak with your local building official—before applying for any permit or beginning construction. We authorize the use of our blueprints on the express condition that you strictly comply with all local building codes, zoning requirements and other applicable laws, regulations, ordinances and requirements. Notice: Plans for homes to be built in Nevada must be re-drawn by a Nevada-registered professional. Consult your building official for more information on this subject.

 TOLL FREE 1-800-521-6797

REGULAR OFFICE HOURS:
8:00 a.m.-9:00 p.m. EST, Monday-Friday

If we receive your order by 3:00 p.m. EST, Monday-Friday, we'll process it and ship within **two business days**. When ordering please have your credit card or check information ready. We'll also ask you for the Order Form Key Number at the bottom of the order form.

By FAX: Copy the Order Form on the next page and send it on our FAX line: 1-800-224-6699 or 520-544-3086.

Canadian Customers
Order Toll Free 1-877-223-6389

ORDER FORM

DISCLAIMER

The designers we work with have put substantial care and effort into the creation of their blueprints. However, because they cannot provide on-site consultation, supervision and control over actual construction, and because of the great variance in local building requirements, building practices and soil, seismic, weather and other conditions, WE CANNOT MAKE ANY WARRANTY, EXPRESS OR IMPLIED, WITH RESPECT TO THE CONTENT OR USE OF THE BLUEPRINTS, INCLUDING BUT NOT LIMITED TO ANY WARRANTY OF MERCHANTABILITY OR OF FITNESS FOR A PARTICULAR PURPOSE. **ITEMS, PRICES, TERMS AND CONDITIONS ARE SUBJECT TO CHANGE WITHOUT NOTICE. REPRODUCIBLE PLAN ORDERS MAY REQUIRE A CUSTOMER'S SIGNED RELEASE BEFORE SHIPPING.**

TERMS AND CONDITIONS

These designs are protected under the terms of United States Copyright Law and may not be copied or reproduced in any way, by any means, unless you have purchased Reproducibles which clearly indicate your right to copy or reproduce. We authorize the use of your chosen design as an aid in the construction of one single family home only. You may not use this design to build a second or multiple dwellings without purchasing another blueprint or blueprints or paying additional design fees.

HOW MANY BLUEPRINTS DO YOU NEED?

Although a standard building package may satisfy many states, cities and counties, some plans may require certain changes. For your convenience, we have developed a Reproducible plan which allows a local professional to modify and make up to 10 copies of your revised plan. As our plans are all copyright protected, with your purchase of the Reproducible, we will supply you with a Copyright release letter. The number of copies you may need: 1 for owner; 3 for builder; 2 for local building department and 1-3 sets for your mortgage lender.

ORDER TOLL FREE!
FOR INFORMATION ABOUT ANY OF OUR SERVICES OR TO ORDER CALL

1-800-521-6797
Browse our website:
www.eplans.com

BLUEPRINTS ARE NOT REFUNDABLE EXCHANGES ONLY

FOR CUSTOMER SERVICE,
CALL TOLL FREE **1-888-690-1116.**

HOME PLANNERS, LLC
Wholly owned by Hanley-Wood, LLC
3275 WEST INA ROAD, SUITE 220 • TUCSON, ARIZONA 85741

THE BASIC BLUEPRINT PACKAGE
Rush me the following (please refer to the Plans Index and Price Schedule in this section):

_____ Set(s) of reproducibles*, plan number(s) _____	$_____
_____ Set(s) of blueprints, plan number(s) _____	$_____
_____ Additional identical blueprints (standard or reverse) in same order @ $50 per set	$_____
_____ Sets of Gazebo Construction Details @ $14.95 per set.	$_____
_____ Sets of Complete Construction Package (Best Buy!) Add $10 to Building Package	
Includes Custom Plan _____	
Plus Deck or Gazebo Construction Details	$_____

IMPORTANT EXTRA
Rush me the following:

Specification Outlines @ $10 each	$_____

POSTAGE AND HANDLING (signature is required for all deliveries)		
CARRIER DELIVERY		
No CODs (Requires street address—No P.O.Boxes)		
• **Regular Service** (Allow 7–10 business days for delivery)	$8.00	$ _____
• **Priority** (Allow 4–5 business days for delivery)	$12.00	$ _____
• **Express** (Allow 3 business days for delivery)	$22.00	$ _____
Overseas Delivery	Phone, FAX or Mail for Quote	

NOTE: All delivery times are from date blueprint package is shipped.

POSTAGE (from box above) $ _____

SUBTOTAL $ _____

SALES TAX (AZ & MI residents, please add appropriate state & local sales tax.) $ _____

TOTAL (Subtotal and Tax) $ _____

YOUR ADDRESS (please print legibly)

Name _____

Street _____

City _____ State _____ ZIP _____

Daytime telephone number (required) _____

* Fax number (required for reproducible orders) _____

TeleCheck® Checks By Phone℠ available

FOR CREDIT CARD ORDERS ONLY Please fill in the information below:

Credit card number_____ Exp: Month/Year _____

Check One: ❏ Visa ❏ MasterCard ❏ American Express

Signature (required) _____

Please check appropriate box: ❏ Licensed Builder-Contractor ❏ Homeowner

ORDER TOLL FREE 1-800-521-6797
BY FAX: Copy the order form above and send it on our FAXLINE:
1-800-224-6699 or 1-520-544-3086

Order Form Key
HPT94

1 BIGGEST & BEST

1001 of our Best-Selling Plans
in One Volume.
1,074 to 7,275 square feet.
704 pgs. $12.95 1K1

2 ONE-STORY

450 designs for all lifestyles.
810 to 5,400 square feet.
448 pgs. $9.95 OS2

3 MORE ONE-STORY

475 Superb One-Level Plans
from 800 to 5,000
square feet.
448 pgs. $9.95 MO2

4 TWO-STORY

450 Best-Selling Designs
for 1½ and 2-stories.
448 pgs. $9.95 TS2

5 VACATION

430 designs for Recreation,
Retirement, and Leisure.
448 pgs. $9.95 VS3

6 HILLSIDE

208 designs for Split-Levels,
Bi-Levels, Multi-Levels,
and Walkouts.
224 pgs. $9.95 HH

7 FARMHOUSE

300 fresh designs from
Classic to Modern.
320 pgs. $10.95 FCP

8 COUNTRY HOUSES

208 unique home plans that
combine Traditional Style and
Modern Livability.
224 pgs. $9.95 CN

9 BUDGET-SMART

200 Efficient Plans from
7 Top Designers, that you can
really afford to build!
224 pgs. $8.95 BS

10 BARRIER-FREE

Over 1,700 products and
51 plans for Accessible Living.
128 pgs. $15.95 UH

11 ENCYCLOPEDIA

500 exceptional plans for all
styles and budgets—
The Best Book of its Kind!
528 pgs. $9.95 ENC3

12 SUN COUNTRY

175 Designs from
Coastal Cottages to
Stunning Southwesterns.
192 pgs. $9.95 SUN

13 AFFORDABLE

300 modest plans
for savvy homebuyers.
256 pgs. $9.95 AH2

14 VICTORIAN

210 striking Victorian and
Farmhouse designs from
today's top designers.
224 pgs. $15.95 VDH2

15 ESTATE

Dream big!
Eighteen designers showcase
their biggest and best plans.
224 pgs. $16.95 EDH3

16 LUXURY

170 lavish designs, over 50%
brand-new plans added to a
most elegant collection.
192 pgs. $12.95 LD3

17 WILLIAM E. POOLE

100 classic house plans from
William E. Poole.
224 pgs. $17.95 WP2

18 HUGE SELECTION

650 home plans—
from Cottages to Mansions
464 pgs. $8.95 650

19 SOUTHWEST

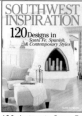

120 designs in Santa Fe,
Spanish, and
Contemporary Styles.
192 pgs. $14.95 SI

20 COUNTRY CLASSICS

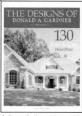

130 Best-Selling Home Plans
from Donald A. Gardner.
192 pgs. $17.95 DAG2

21 COTTAGES

245 Delightful retreats from
825 to 3,500 square feet.
256 pgs. $10.95 COOL

22 CONTEMPORARY

The most complete and
imaginative collection of
contemporary designs available.
256 pgs. $10.95 CM2

23 FRENCH COUNTRY

Live every day in the French
countryside using these plans,
landscapes and interiors.
192 pgs. $14.95 PN

24 SOUTHWESTERN

138 designs that capture the
spirit of the Southwest.
144 pgs. $10.95 SW

25 SHINGLE-STYLE

155 home plans from
Classic Colonials to
Breezy Bungalows.
192 pgs. $12.95 SNG

26 NEIGHBORHOOD

170 designs with the feel
of main street America.
192 pgs. $12.95 TND

27 CRAFTSMAN

170 Home plans in the
Craftsman and Bungalow
style. 192 pgs. $12.95 CC

28 GRAND VISTAS

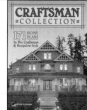

200 Homes with a View.
224 pgs. $10.95 GV

29 MULTI-FAMILY

115 Duplex, Multiplex &
Townhome Designs.
128 pgs. $17.95 MFH

30 WATERFRONT

200 designs perfect for your
Waterside Wonderland.
208 pgs. $10.95 WF

Home Planners wants your building experience to be as pleasant and trouble-free as possible. That's why we've expanded our library of do-it-yourself titles to help you along.

31 NATURAL LIGHT

223 Sunny home plans for all regions.
240 pgs. $8.95 NA

32 NOSTALGIA

100 Time-Honored designs updated with today's features.
224 pgs. $14.95 NOS

33 DREAM HOMES

50 luxury home plans. Over 300 illustrations.
256 pgs. $19.95 SOD2

34 NARROW-LOT

245 versatile designs up to 50 feet wide.
256 pgs. $9.95 NL2

35 SMALL HOUSES

Innovative plans for sensible lifestyles.
224 pgs. $8.95 SM2

36 OUTDOOR

74 easy-to-build designs, lets you create and build your own backyard oasis.
128 pgs. $9.95 YG2

37 GARAGES

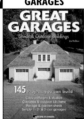

145 exciting projects from 64 to 1,900 square feet.
160 pgs. $9.95 GG2

38 PLANNER

A Planner for Building or Remodeling your Home.
318 pgs. $17.95 SCDH

39 HOME BUILDING

Everything you need to know to work with contractors and subcontractors.
212 pgs. $14.95 HBP

40 RURAL BUILDING

Everything you need to know to build your home in the country.
232 pgs. $14.95 BYC

41 VACATION HOMES

Your complete guide to building your vacation home.
224 pgs. $14.95 BYV

42 DECKS

A brand new collection of 120 beautiful and practical decks.
144 pgs. $9.95 DP2

43 GARDENS & MORE

225 gardens, landscapes, decks and more to enhance every home.
320 pgs. $19.95 GLP

44 EASY-CARE

41 special landscapes designed for beauty and low maintenance.
160 pgs. $14.95 ECL

45 BACKYARDS

40 designs focused solely on creating your own specially themed backyard oasis.
160 pgs. $14.95 BYL

46 BEDS & BORDERS

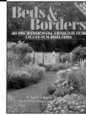

40 Professional designs for do-it-yourselfers
160 pgs. $14.95 BB

Adaptable and easy to grow, Asiatic lilies star in this mid-summer flower garden.